THE INDOOR CLIMBING MANUAL

JOHN WHITE

BLOOMSBURY

Note While every effort has been made to ensure that the content of this book is as technically accurate and as sound as possible, neither the author nor the publishers can accept responsibility for any injury or loss sustained as a result of the use of this material.

Published by Bloomsbury Publishing Plc
50 Bedford Square
London WC1B 3DP
www.bloomsbury.com

First edition 2013

ISBN (print): 978-1-4081-8662-6
ISBN (ePdf): 978-1-4081-8663-3
ISBN (EPUB): 978-1-4081-8664-0

A CIP catalogue record for this book is available from the British Library.

Acknowledgements
Cover and inside photography by John White, Dave Willis, Paddy Cave, Philippe Galland and Aimee Roseborrough, further inside photography from Getty Images, Press Association Images, Heiko Wilhelm and Risk4Sport, see page 4 for full information. For any photography not credited please contact Bloomsbury.

Designed by Austin Taylor

This book is produced using paper that is made from wood grown in managed, sustainable forests. It is natural, renewable and recyclable. The logging and manufacturing processes conform to the environmental regulations of the country of origin.

Typeset in The Serif Light

Printed and bound in China by C&C Offset Printing Co

10 9 8 7 6 5 4 3 2 1

Contents

ACKNOWLEDGEMENTS

Researching and writing this book has been an immense amount of fun. I've made some new friends and reacquainted myself with lots of old ones, and they've all been so helpful and generous with their time.

I'd particularly like to thank the following people for providing equipment and expertise, for modelling (and sometimes posing) and for freely providing advice and ideas. In no particular order: Dave Birkett, Iain 'Wilf's Cafe' Williamson and friends – Ray Farrager, Andy Tilney and Kerry Bumby, Luke White, Elliot White, Ellen Spencer and Anna, Nick Wharton, Neil Cooper (The 'Fall Guy'), Evolv sponsored climbers Adam Lincoln and Nick Moulden, Morgan Weymouth and family, Dave Willis, Richard Bailey, Will and Bill Birkett, Derek and Janet Capper.

Paul Cornforth at King Kong Climbing Walls, Kate Phillips and all the staff at Kendal Wall (Lakeland Climbing Centre), Rick at Evolv footwear, Lyon Equipment, Beal and Petzl, and several other climbing walls for being kind enough to allow photos to be taken including Reading, Milton Keynes, Northampton (especially Tom), Redpoint Birmingham, The Ice Factor, The Castle and The Arch, Aimee Roseborrough and Maureen Flett for invaluable help with the section on climbing injuries, Adrian Baxter of ClimbCoach for assistance with the chapter on training and to the many other climbers whose names I don't know or have forgotten ... thanks!

Image credits Photography by John White, Dave Willis, Paddy Cave, Philippe Galland, Aimee Roseborrough. Further photography:
Pages 4 and 159 © Shutterstock
Page 6 © Romilly Lockyer/Getty Images
Page 13 © King Kong Climbing Walls
Page 14 © Tom Bol/Getty Images
Page 32 © Marvin E. Newman/Getty Images
Page 42 © Ty Allison/Getty Images
Pages 64 and 132 © Image Source/Getty Images
Page 92 © Aurora Open/Getty Images
Pages 166 and 172 (bottom) © Luka Dakskobler/
    Demotix/Press Association Images
Page 168 © Heiko Wilhelm
Page 169 © Luca Parisse/Risk4Sport
Page 170 © Larry Clouse/Landov/Press Association Images
Page 171 © Miguel Medina/Stringer/AFP/Getty Images
Pages 171 (bottom right), 172 (top) and 173
    © Peter Scholz/Demotix/Press Association Images

Introduction
A BRIEF HISTORY OF ROCK CLIMBING

Climbing indoors has undergone a revolution since the first purpose-built indoor climbing walls were built in the 1960s and 1970s. In climbing terms it's a revolution on par with that experienced in the mid-1900s, when rock climbing went from being the preserve of the wealthy to a working man's sport.

Gone are the days when an indoor wall was simply a means to an end – used to learn a few practical skills and help outdoor climbers get a bit fitter for what was called 'the real thing'.

Through the 1980s and 1990s, indoor climbing walls continued to act as catalysts for improvements in outdoor climbing standards – but a new breed of climber was also emerging, focused simply on the gymnastic and competitive elements offered by indoor climbing.

Many exponents of indoor climbing started to shun the traditional forms of climbing, opting for the security of bolt-protected, weatherproof climbs indoors, and for bouldering. The high cost of travelling to, and staying at, outdoor climbing areas has been a contributory factor as well – not to mention the price of the equipment.

By the first decade of the new millennium, indoor climbing walls were springing up everywhere, from primary schools and universities to massive, purpose-built centres offering hundreds of climbs and dedicated training facilities.

The most recent developments have included a proliferation of bouldering-only centres, appealing to those seeking an alternative way of keeping fit as well as to dedicated boulderers. Perhaps the most interesting fact of all is the proportion of this new breed of climbers who actually climb outside on real rock: many modern facilities report that between 70 and 90 per cent of their users do not climb outside at all.

What a contrast with the early days of climbing walls, when an estimated 95 per cent of users climbed outside as well!

1

A HISTORY OF CLIMBING WALLS

with assistance from
Paul Cornforth of King
Kong Climbing Walls

The history of artificial climbing walls probably starts in the 1930s with the construction of an artificial climbing wall out of doors – the Schurman Rock, built at Camp Long, a Scout Camp near Seattle, from giant boulders of real rock.

This was the birth of the concept of creating something artificial to climb and to train on. Training here refers to technical training such as learning to belay, manage ropes and hold falls and learning to climb specific climbing features such as cracks or friction slabs, rather than training to improve performance.

As a fantastic example of how an artificial climbing wall can inspire people, 12-year-old twin brothers Lou and James Whittaker did their first climbs on the Rock in 1941. In 1963 James Whittaker went on to make the first American ascent of Mount Everest. Not to be outdone, the following year, his brother Lou made the first ascent of the North Col of Everest.

▼ The Schurman Rock, Seattle

Prior to the construction of the first artificial climbing walls in Britain, climbers used buildings and other artificial structures to train on. A classic example can be seen in the Abraham Brothers' photo of 19th-century mountaineer Owen Glynne Jones on the unmistakable Barn Door Traverse at Wasdale Head in the Lake District.

Students at Cambridge University famously used the heavily featured walls of the colleges for climbing and there is little doubt that the walls of bridges, viaducts and many other man-made structures would have been climbed for practice once the post-war boom in rock climbing began.

▲ The Barn Door Traverse at Wasdale Head, the Lake District

THE FIRST CLIMBING WALLS

Some basic wooden climbing walls were built in France in the 1950s, but when and where was the first artificial climbing wall constructed in Britain? It seems likely that it was in 1960 at Ullswater School in Penrith on the outskirts of the Lake District. Here, a climbing wall, basic in modern terms and created by a mix of protruding and inset brickwork with brick and concrete ledges, was built in the gym. Ten years later a new gym was constructed at the school and a new wall was built, this time outside, illustrating that the architects responsible clearly did not understand the temperamental Cumbrian weather!

The next developments were typified by the iconic Leeds Wall, which used natural rock holds cemented into the brickwork. This was the first wall to be constructed simply for training in a physical sense, and regular users of the wall were able to develop levels of fitness that improved local climbing standards significantly.

John Syrett, probably the most famous of the Leeds Wall climbers, adopted the types of intensive training now used in modern climbing. He spent a year developing his strength and technical skill on the Leeds Wall. Although he rarely climbed outside, in 1970 he started climbing on real rock and made some difficult first ascents, including Joker's Wall (E4 6a) at Brimham Rocks, possibly his most famous climb.

The first commercial wall

Don Robinson of DR Climbing Walls built the first commercial climbing wall in 1964. These early artificial walls were usually designed by climbers, for climbers, and their sole purpose was as a training tool for use in the long winter months and on wet days when it was either impossible or too unpleasant to venture outside. As such most of them were fairly fierce, with sharp holds made either from cement or from natural rock cemented into a concrete block, along with moulded cracks and holds.

The idea at this time was to emulate the kind of climbing one would experience outside in the 'real' world, and some of these early walls did a pretty good job of it. However, their greatest weakness was that you couldn't change the layout of the holds and routes without significant work and great expense.

⌄ The Ullswater School wall can still be seen from the road into Penrith – standing proud and unused on the end of the school gym

⌄ Leeds Climbing Wall

▲ The advent of colour-coded bolt-on holds was to revolutionise the design of indoor climbing walls

climbs and it was possible to have an 8a grade climb next to a 4b just by adding smaller (or larger) holds.

There was still a demand to make walls that emulated natural rock and generally this was achieved by a system widely known as 'Freeform'. This is a resinous cement system that when in use has the malleable qualities of clay but when cured sets rock solid. This is normally added to the final coating of a GRP wall and is hand sculpted. However, one of the problems with Freeform is that it is only as good as the sculptor forming the holds. If the user is skilled at forming the features found in natural rock then it can look spectacular. The flip side is that if the sculptor is a non-artistic non-climber it can end up looking very amateurish and be awful to climb on. Design is everything.

The advent of bolt-on holds also heralded the development of home training facilities – characterised by the 'cellar-dweller' developments of Sheffield climbers, but appearing countrywide in garages, outbuildings and other similar structures.

BOLT-ON HOLDS

This design of climbing walls continued in a similar vein until the mid-1980s and the introduction of the 'bolt-on hold', which dramatically changed the look, design and feel of climbing walls. Whereas all walls before this time had fixed holds sculpted into the wall surface and were impossible to change or vary, the bolt-on hold allowed the climbing to be changed very easily and so grades of climbs could be readily adjusted. It also introduced the concept of colour-coded climbs – a revolutionary factor in terms of the development of indoor climbing.

It wasn't just the holds that changed. Lighter climbing panels were introduced using Plywood and GRP (glass-reinforced plastic) as a base, with a rich matrix of possible bolt-on hold sites on the panels. This provided even more scope to vary the

▼ An outdoor King Kong Freeform wall at Bosworth Academy provides ideal traversing

➤ DIY bouldering walls became very popular with the advent of bolt-on holds

➤ Looking up the 25m main wall at Kendal

HEIGHT ISN'T EVERYTHING

By the 1990s there seemed to be a race on to build the tallest wall in the country, as if height was the most important requirement for a climbing wall. The Marple Wall, in Stockport, was 18m high, the old Birmingham Wall (now closed) was also around 18m high and in 1994 Kendal Wall in the Lake District opened at 20m high. In Scotland, Ratho went one better and built a 25m-high wall in one of the most outrageous climbing wall projects ever undertaken. It involved constructing a roof over a disused quarry and creating artificial walls alongside the natural stone of the quarry. It was a massive undertaking, intended as a centre for various other sports as well as the location of a 50-room hotel and a shopping mall. Unfortunately the company behind it went bankrupt when the wall had only been open for a couple of months. Costs for the venture had spiralled out of control, reputedly reaching a staggering £27 million. The centre was then bought by Edinburgh Council and is now run as the Edinburgh International Climbing Centre (EICC).

But is bigger necessarily better? A lot of people who were visiting the new walls weren't dedicated climbers and the effect of this was that the most challenging, overhanging, highest walls weren't getting anywhere near as much traffic as walls of a more modest height. Consequently wall designs have had to change to cater for this shift in user ability. Climbing walls are now being built for mid-grade climbers in order to attract the masses, and to some extent the dedicated climbers are a secondary consideration.

Some walls still maintain their appeal to serious climbers: Kate Phillips, Kendal Wall's manager, reports that an increasing number of younger climbers are using the 25m-high main wall. High walls also have a very useful part to play in replicating the sustained effort required for both longer climbs and competition climbing.

▲ All very civilised at a modern bouldering centre –
The Arch, London

NEW WAVE

The development of climbing walls continued throughout the 1990s and 2000s, often combining shop and café facilities with a mix of lead climbing, top roping and bouldering walls to create dedicated climbing facilities. Competition climbing increased in popularity, too, and this spawned numerous bouldering competitions ranging from local bouldering ladders to full international competitions. Into the 2010s, the development of walls shows no sign of slowing.

The sport of bouldering has long been popular with climbers and many have visited the likes of the world-famous bouldering mecca of Fontainebleau just south of Paris. While bouldering walls have always been deemed an essential part of a serious dedicated climbing centre, the Climbing Works, in Sheffield, made the brave move of opening a dedicated bouldering centre with no roped climbing. This had never been done before on such a grand scale and has proved highly successful with climbers. The upshot is that many more dedicated bouldering walls have opened up in the UK. Bouldering-only centres make good commercial sense. They are much easier to manage than a roped climbing wall; cheaper to run; cheaper to build; and cheaper to insure. The age profile of visitors is also significantly different to that of most leading walls, and many modern bouldering-wall users don't climb outside on real rock, simply using climbing as a great way to keep fit. This has dramatically increased participation levels, but leads to the question: how sustainable will it be without further evolution?

THE FUTURE OF CLIMBING WALLS

So, from a real climbing perspective, what does the future hold?

If the trend continues for quick-fix, adrenalin-rush activities for the general public then the development of artificial climbing walls will continue to reflect this.

The gap between natural outdoor climbing and indoor climbing will widen and diversify still further. A company with its roots in New Zealand called Clip 'N Climb has taken this idea to a new level. All climbs are protected by automatic belay devices and various climbing elements that resemble high ropes course challenges; these are brightly painted and wouldn't look out of place on a funfair. Participants navigate a range of problems, including rope swings, climbing on spinning holds, climbing with Velcro gloves, and so on. It has proved incredibly popular and it's easy to see why as it's a lot of fun, but it remains to be seen if it is sustainable in the long term. These centres are the kind of places that someone might visit once or twice, but because the challenges are easily met, they don't provide the in-depth challenge that a more serious climber needs.

In the classic climbing film *Stone Monkey*, starring Johnny Dawes, a different type of climbing is presented, one that is really dynamic and springy and in a lot of ways like the new sport of 'parkour' or 'street running'. Several street-running parks have opened recently and there is a definite crossover between climbing and street running, which may mean that some bouldering centres have a dedicated parkour area in the future.

Over the last 20 years the trend has switched from walls that have tried to resemble natural climbing outside to a sterile version of climbing with minimal risk, without sharp holds and in a lot of ways without the technical difficulties that are experienced outside. About 99 per cent of all bolt-on holds can be easily used as footholds even if they are poor handholds and a new system of holds would go a long way towards bringing climbing styles closer again to the complexities of climbing on real rock. Volumes and bolt-on features have long been popular and they have definitely added interest to the climbing experience.

▲ King Kong Climbing Walls' Walkers Deep Ridged Climbing Crisp

Recently, climbing wall panels have become much more complex in shape, with multi-faceted surfaces becoming the norm. This trend will continue and even wackier 'space age' designs might soon be seen.

As the sport of ice climbing becomes more popular, it's likely that more pure ice-climbing walls will open and as the sport of bouldering continues to go from strength to strength more dedicated bouldering walls will emerge.

The future inclusion of climbing as an Olympic sport will also herald changes, with walls having to adapt to the types of walls, boulder problems and training facilities required for international Olympic competitions.

The sport of indoor climbing has fragmented and diversified progressively in the last 20 years, and the traditional roped lead wall is only a part of the wider sport of artificial climbing that now includes bouldering centres, funfair-type climbing, ice climbing and parkour.

Watch this space!

◄ Clip n' Climb offer a very different climbing experience!

EQUIPMENT FOR CLIMBING INDOORS

In comparison to outdoor climbing, you don't need a lot of kit for climbing indoors – in fact you could go bouldering on an indoor wall with no specialist equipment whatsoever as many walls rent out basic equipment, such as rock shoes and harnesses.

Having the right equipment will help you climb better and more safely and, if you intend to start roped climbing, rather than bouldering, you'll need more equipment and a thorough understanding of how to choose it and use it.

Here's a summary of what you're going to need according to the type of climbing you'll be doing.

BOULDERING

For bouldering you'll need rock shoes to help you to better use the smaller and sloping holds.

You'll also need a chalk bag and some chalk, which will help provide a better grip for your hands – especially on smaller or sloping holds. Most climbing walls stipulate that you should use chalk balls rather than the loose blocks, which create dust.

You'll feel more comfortable in loose-fitting clothes, which will allow you unrestricted movement.

TOP ROPE CLIMBING

As well as some rock shoes and a chalk bag, for top rope climbing you'll also need a harness, belay device and carabiner. Once again, clothing allowing freedom of movement is essential.

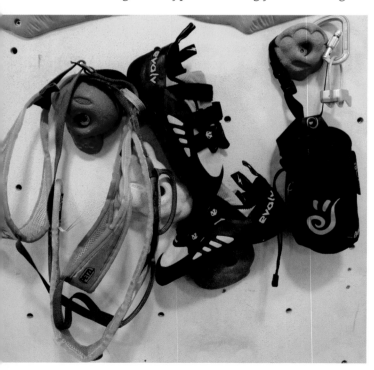

◄ For top-rope climbing you'll need a harness and belay device to go along with your rock shoes and chalk bag

▲ You don't need much gear for bouldering – a chalk bag and rock shoes is about it

LEAD CLIMBING

When you start to lead climb, you'll need the equipment and clothing previously mentioned, plus a rope and some quickdraws (see full details below).

THE GEAR – A CLOSER LOOK

Rock shoes

You'll find yourself at an instant disadvantage if you're not wearing rock shoes, as the difference they make is immense. Take a look at a pair and you'll observe several key characteristics.

The soles are smooth, with a round-the-foot rand, heel and toe piece that provide a complete gripping surface around the foot. The rubber is specially created to give maximum friction.

The shape is also unlike that of an ordinary trainer. The toe is narrow and the laces run right down to the toe to give maximum control. On Velcro-fastening shoes, the shape of the laces provides much of the stability and the Velcro is positioned to give a precise fit. The heel cup is pronounced and deep, while the sole is often curved the opposite way to your normal foot shape, an asymmetric last shape that improves the fit and performance. The shoes are also very light and, finally, you may notice that size for size, they look very small!

▼ A very small foothold requires rock shoes

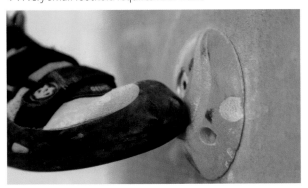

All these design factors together create a shoe that grips supremely well, is tight fitting, hugs your foot without any play whatsoever and allows the easiest possible transition of force from your body to the foothold.

CHOOSING ROCK SHOES

- Many walls rent out rock boots – this could be the best way for you to try them out.
- The correct fit is more important than appearance or brand.
- What are you buying them for? Bouldering, slabs, overhanging routes?
- What's your budget?
- Look at reviews in climbing magazines and information on websites to help you choose.
- Talking to other climbers might help as well.
- When buying your first pair, make sure that the shoe fits your foot shape as closely as possible. Do your fitting in bare feet. Try on a few different pairs and feel the difference.
- Go to a shop with a good reputation and a large selection of makes and models.
- Don't shop for rock shoes on the internet – you have to try them on.
- Don't buy rock shoes too big – you may be able to wear them comfortably all evening, but you won't be able to get the precision required when using smaller footholds.
- Cramming your toes into an extremely tight shoe for long periods of time can cause permanent damage to your toes – particularly in children, whose feet are growing and developing. I can clearly recall thinking many times that there should be a special word for the feeling you get when you take off your over-tight rock shoes after a long climb!

Rock shoes for your purpose

Here's what Rick from Beyond Hope, the importers of Evolv rock shoes, says about choosing rock shoes:

Rock shoes are designed with a specific 'last' around which the shoe is constructed. This is designed to manipulate the shape of the foot into the best climbing shape. Depending on how 'technical' a shoe is, last shapes will vary depending on how much the foot is manipulated.

In extreme cases, shoes for very specific, overhanging routes and problems tend to have an almost claw-like appearance, with last shapes designed to help the climber pull their bodyweight closer to the wall and stand on very small edges or pockets. Rock shoe shapes will vary between those that are more 'normal' and, therefore, comfortable and those that are more extreme.

The temptation for many newer climbers is to buy into more technical shoe offerings in the assumption it will make them climb harder. However, this is often a mistake as the more technical shoes tend to offer less comfort and are also highly specific to a certain style of climbing.

▾ It's a great feeling getting those rock shoes off!

▸ A range of rock shoes on offer at Kendal Wall's shop

Rock shoes also vary in the rubber compounds used. These days, virtually all the rock boot manufacturers will use a 'sticky' rubber, and the differences between brands are probably smaller than many would think!

When buying a pair of shoes, be honest about what you need. Go to a recommended retailer and ask the staff for advice on the models that are suitable. Fit is crucial. You should fill the inside of the shoe, with minimal 'dead space'. Toes should not just reach the end – they should be at least slightly bent. The heel cup should be filled and secure when heel-hooking. Try on a variety and ignore the size printed on the box –there is an enormous amount of variety between brands and even within ranges, so your normal shoe size can only really be used as a starting point.

Chalk bag and chalk

The use of 'chalk' – light magnesium carbonate – makes a significant difference as it improves your grip. Choose a chalk bag you can get your hand into comfortably and that has an easy to fasten drawstring. Beyond that it's simply a case of style and taste. Wall staff will often ask you to use chalk balls rather than blocks, since the latter produces more dust in the air. Although this makes sense, I still love the feel of crumbling a block of chalk into the bag. There may be serious health issues related to using blocks, however: climbing wall workers and climbers spend a lot of time at the walls, exposed to chalk dust over extended periods, and it's not clear whether there is likely to be any long-term damage to a person's health as a result. Save your chalk blocks for outdoor climbing!

Harness

The harness provides a safe means of attaching the climbing rope, belay and abseil device to the climber and, in the event of a fall, ensures that the forces involved are spread as comfortably as possible through the climber's waist, lower back and upper legs, via the waist belt and leg loops.

There are many makes and models, and they all work. However, there are subtle differences and you should consider the following information when making your choice.

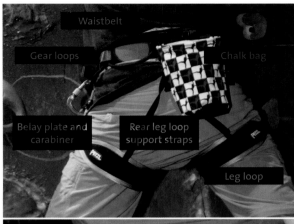

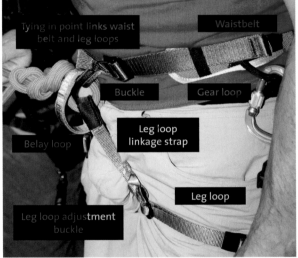

▲ The main features of a typical modern climbing harness

The most common type of harness has a waist belt and two leg loops, linked at the front by a belay loop and at the back by lightweight straps, which hold the leg loops up. They also have plastic loops attached to the waist belt, onto which other equipment can be clipped.

◄ Group harness with pre-threaded buckles: simply pull the belt to tighten. Note the horizontal belay loop and lack of gear loops – a disadvantage once you move on from the beginner's stage

▲ The pre-threaded waist belt lacks gear loops

▲ Quickdraws clipped to gear loops. More gear carrying is available on the other side of the harness and on the rear.

The waist belt can be of two main types: those with a buckle through which you have to thread the waist belt; and those which have a pre-threaded buckle that you simply pull to tighten. The majority of harnesses now feature the pre-threaded type.

Climbing harness waist belts are generally padded, apart from the cheaper 'group use' type of harness, and this makes them more comfortable to wear and to lower/fall into. The amount of padding and width of the belt varies, so this is one of the factors to take into account when you are buying.

The leg loops are padded and can be adjustable or non-adjustable. Either will be acceptable for indoor use, though for outdoor use you may prefer the versatility afforded by adjustable leg loops.

Gear loops on waist belts also vary in size, number and configuration. For indoor climbing you need to be able to reach them easily on both sides. Check that they are positioned correctly for you

when you have the correct size of harness.

The size of the harness is important as it relates to the position of the gear loops, and to overall fit. The variables here are in relation to waist belt and leg loop size and also take into consideration the relationship between the waist belt and leg loops. The waist belt, when fastened at the correct tension – that is, a couple of thumbs fitting down between you and the belt, but not enough space to slide your hands down – should use approximately two-thirds to one-half of the available adjustment. This allows for both a bit of expansion due to the use of different clothing you might wear outside, for example, and a little contraction when you shed a couple of kilos through your climbing exertions!

The gear loops should be in an easy-to-reach position to the side. The leg loops should be snug but not too tight. Loose leg loops will place too much force on the waist belt in the event of a fall, rather than the force being shared with the upper legs.

If you find a harness that is the right fit and the right price then carry out one final check by asking the shop to let you try sitting in the harness. All good climbing shops will have a sling set up so you can clip into it and do this. You should find the harness puts you comfortably in a sitting position. If not, readjust or try a different one.

For younger children, a full-body harness is recommended. This type of harness has a higher centre of gravity to help prevent any possibility of turning upside down. Younger children often have very little hip/waist differentiation, and standard sit harnesses can slip down – another problem overcome by the use of a full body harness.

Finally, do not buy cheaper 'group use'

⌄ A full body harness is recommended for younger children

➤ A belay plate in use

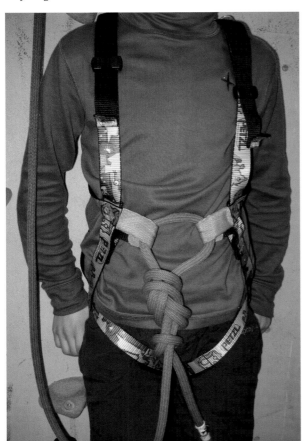

beginners' harnesses. These are often not padded, have few gear loops and, more importantly, do not have a vertical belay loop on the front. As your climbing progresses you will find this type of design has limitations.

Belay device

A belay device attaches to the belayer's harness and is used primarily to control the fall of the climber – whether top roping or leading – and to lower a climber to the ground. Many belay devices can also be used to abseil with.

They can be subdivided into two main categories: belay plates and Grigri-type auto-locking devices – both of which require the belayer to hold the rope in order for them to lock. Grigri-type devices usually incorporate some sort of camming device that locks the rope when it is subjected to the sudden force of a fall.

Belay plates are mostly made with two slots, so

▲ A sample selection of belay devices

you can use a single or a double rope (often used in outdoor climbing). Some belay plates are specially designed for sport climbing and will just take a single rope. If you're ever likely to need to abseil, you should buy a belay plate with two slots, as abseiling is normally undertaken on a double rope.

A standard belay plate allows you to take in the rope easily while someone is top rope climbing and to pay out rope and make rapid, minor adjustments when someone is lead climbing. It also allows you to lock the device to hold a top rope or leader and to lower someone to the ground. Additionally, you can abseil with the device.

How do belay devices work?

Belaying plates use a combination of friction and a pinching effect (controlled in turn by the user's arm position and grip) to produce a braking force on the rope. The type of effect most used depends on the design of the device. Devices relying to a greater extent on friction will tend to be smooth running and require the belayer to react speedily by providing the right controlling action on the rope.

Belay plates giving a greater pinch effect will tend to grab the rope and lock up under load as the plate is pulled against the carabiner, but they still require careful and controlled use. They can be much more difficult to use when paying out the rope to a lead climber due to the tendency of the rope to lock up, but do provide a better locking action in the event of a fall. This type of device is today less popular than it used to be.

With no moving parts, belay plates rely on the user to provide the correct arm/rope positions and correct gripping force to produce a braking effect.

Some belay devices operate solely by pinching or camming the rope; an example of this is the Petzl Grigri. These types of device lock when loaded suddenly and provide a very high level of security. The term auto-locking is slightly misleading, as the devices still require action from the belayer to be used correctly. They are advised for use by more experienced belayers.

In practice, these are very popular with sport climbers. Following a fall, the device locks and although you need to keep hold of the rope, you don't have to apply the same level of grip to the rope to hold the climber in position. Lowering a climber is achieved through moving a lever to reduce the device's grip on the rope. Such devices can only be used with single ropes and are used mostly in sport climbing. They are significantly more expensive than a standard belay plate, but are very popular.

◀ Grigri 2 in action

An 'auto-locking' belay device should lock when subjected to a sudden loading; this makes them very popular with experienced sport climbers. Once locked, the device should remain so until released by the belayer, making it easier to manage the situation when lead climbers are falling and resting.

One of the key factors to consider when choosing a belay plate is the type and thickness of rope you'll be using it with. Different devices work with different thicknesses of ropes. This information is presented with the device at the point of sale and if you're not sure do ask for expert advice.

If you get the relationship between belay device and rope wrong you could end up with difficulties feeding the rope through the plate, if it is too thick, or with problems holding falls and lowering, if it is too thin.

The following factors should be taken into account when choosing and using a belay plate:

- The thickness and slickness of ropes to be used.
- The weight of the climber.
- The experience level of the user.
- The single or double rope use.
- Whether it's going to be used for indoor or outdoor/indoor combination.

For indoor wall climbers, the most popular devices for beginners are the standard belay plates such as Petzl Verso, Wild Country VC Pro and Black Diamond ATC. Experienced users also go for these types, with many also opting for the auto-locking devices such as the Petzl Grigri or Edelrid Eddy. Instructors will often be seen with the Petzl Reverso or Black Diamond ATC Guide.

Choosing the right device reduces the chance of an accident while belaying or lowering, and makes for a smoother climb. However, any device needs to be properly operated in order to be effective, so it's essential to make sure you know how to use it, pay attention and remember that your climbing partner is relying on you!

Belay carabiner

All belay devices have to link to your harness via a carabiner. This carabiner must have a locking gate to prevent any accidental opening. If you use a normal screwgate carabiner, you must ensure that it is of the pear/HMS shape. You must also ensure that when using this combination, you are careful to ensure that the carabiner remains loaded correctly at all times, with the rope at the wider end of the carabiner and its narrower end at the belay loop. It is possible for the carabiner to flip round 90 degrees so that it is cross-loaded and, thus, significantly weaker.

▲ A standard screwgate belay carabiner

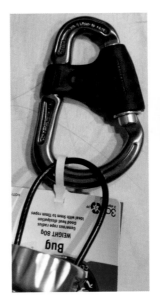

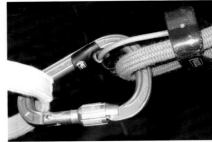

◄ A DMM belay carabiner with plastic clip separating harness attachment point from rope attachment point to keep the carabiner loaded correctly

▲ The Petzl system of a sliding plastic clip holds the carabiner in place and prevents rotating or cross-loading

To prevent this happening, you can buy carabiners with different methods of retaining the equipment in the correct position. A plastic clip may be used to split the carabiner into two sections so it cannot rotate, and Petzl have developed the Universo belay device, which uses a plastic clip system to lock the belay plate into position on the carabiner. Not only does this prevent accidental rotation and possible cross-loading, but it also helps prevent you dropping the belay plate accidentally when climbing outdoors.

Rope

You'll encounter a wide range of situations at different climbing walls. Some walls have lots of fixed ropes, while others have very few. Typically, walls have both leading and fixed rope areas.

Your choice of rope, as with many other items of equipment, depends on a range of factors. For example, are you going to use the rope for both indoor and outdoor climbing? How long are the routes you want to climb? Are you a beginner or more experienced? Whatever your answers to these questions, here's the lowdown on climbing ropes.

The first thing to understand is that climbing ropes stretch when a load is placed on them. This 'dynamic' property allows the rope to dissipate some of the energy created when a fall occurs. The rope forms part of the 'fall arrest' system that links the climber to the belayer through the harness and belay plate.

If, for example, you climbed on a steel cable and fell, there would be no elasticity in the system and the shock loading in the event of a fall would be massive, resulting in failure of another part of the system and/or injury to the climber. If you climbed on a bungee, you'd get lots of shock-absorbing elasticity – too much, in fact – and you'd probably end up on the ground! A climbing rope offers a shock-absorbing ability somewhere between these two extremes.

Climbing ropes are divided into two key categories – single ropes and half ropes. Sport climbers usually use single ropes, particularly for indoor climbing. One further category is low-stretch or static ropes. These are designed primarily for abseiling and for ascending – as practised in caving, for example. They are not designed for lead climbing and such use would be dangerous, as the rope cannot absorb the force created in a leader fall, resulting in much higher loading on all other parts of the fall arrest system.

All climbing ropes are described as 'Kernmantle' – meaning that they are constructed with a core (kern) and an outer sheath (mantle). The core provides the majority of the rope's strength and consists of thousands of fibres braided into strands, which in turn are braided into bigger and thicker strands that run the full length of the rope. The thickness of the sheath as a proportion of the rope's diameter may vary. Thicker sheaths wear better. The sheath may also be dry treated; that is, impregnated with a water repellent. This may make the rope slightly more difficult to handle as it is slicker, but it can also increase longevity.

▼ Close-up showing Kernmantle structure and rope interior

SINGLE ROPES

Single ropes are the norm for indoor and sport climbing and are often used for single-pitch and lower-grade outdoor climbs. Any rope marked as a single rope is designed to be used on its own, singly between the climbers, though you could use the thinner ones as a half rope.

Single ropes range from 11mm in diameter at the thick end of the spectrum, down to 8.9mm in diameter at the thinnest end.

For repeated use on outdoor climbs, 11mm ropes are good, especially on rough rock such as gritstone, as their extra thickness helps them to withstand wear and tear better. They are slightly heavier than thinner ropes, however.

A very thin 8.9mm rope is used for high-standard sport climbing, where rope weight and friction reduction (through protection points) are important factors.

For most beginners – whether involved in indoor or outdoor climbing – a single rope with a diameter of 10, 10.2 or 10.5mm is ideal.

HALF ROPES

Thinner ropes, designated as half ropes, are not designed to be used singly; use two together. Normally used for longer outdoor routes, the two ropes give a longer retrievable abseil, coupled with much better protection possibilities on more complex routes, with a reduction in rope friction/drag and lower impact forces.

Half ropes were traditionally 9mm in diameter, but it's now possible to get them at a 7.8mm diameter, which feels a bit like washing line! The latter are not really used in indoor climbing.

ROPE LABELS

All ropes are labelled with certain standard information, including the diameter and whether the rope is designed for use as a single or half rope. The following information is also found:

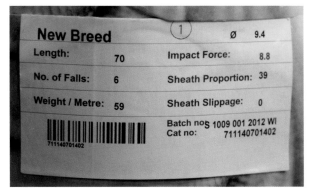

▲ A typical rope label, showing diameter, length, impact force and falls held

Length Ropes normally start at 50m and go up to 70m. Most walls are 20m high or less, so a 50m rope is more than adequate. On 25m walls, you'd need a 55m or 60m rope to allow for safe lowering off. Outdoor sport routes could be longer.

Falls held A standard drop test measures how many falls a rope will hold before breaking. A rope must withstand at least five of these standard falls. The higher this figure is, the better you'll probably feel about your rope, though no rope is a dud! The ability of a rope to absorb shock and hold falls reduces with age, exposure to UV light, dirt and moisture.

Impact force This is important – it's a reflection of the rope's ability to absorb energy. The lower the figure, the less shock-loading the climber – and the protection holding them – is exposed to. This is relevant to outdoor climbing, particularly as the less force applied to protection, the better chance it has of holding.

Weight The weight of the rope in grams per metre will be displayed, giving you a clear idea of the relative weights of different ropes.

Looking after your rope – coiling

It's wise to coil your rope correctly to avoid snags, jams and knots. There are two main methods. First, using a rope bag, you can simply lay your rope in the bag, feeding it in lengths to fit the bag and being careful not to impart any twists into the rope. You may find loops on the bag onto which you can tie the bottom end and the top end of the rope so they don't get lost in the coils. When you've finished, you can fasten your rope bag up and the next time you go climbing, you simply open the bag and the rope will uncoil cleanly straight out of it. This is a great way of using and storing your rope for indoor climbing.

The second method is a coiling method used by most climbers for outdoor climbing and perfectly suitable for indoor climbers as well. Outdoors, this method has the advantage that it makes the rope easy to carry and easy to set up for abseils, plus, if you do it right, it will always uncoil smoothly and tangle free.

The method is called 'Alpine style' and you start by taking the two ends of the rope together and then by pulling through about 4m and laying this on the ground. You then lay the rope backwards and forwards over your outstretched hand – this lays the rope instead of coiling it – until you reach the end. (You can also lay the rope backwards and forwards over your shoulders, which requires less strength.) You can then go back to the 4m you laid to one side and use this to bind the rope, leaving enough rope left over to enable you to carry the rope on your back, rucksack style.

I would advise against coiling the rope round and round in coils – if anyone undoes the rope from the end it was originally coiled, you'll end up with twist after twist – rather like those annoying kinks you get in hosepipes.

When uncoiling a brand new rope, be very careful to follow the instructions (assuming there are any). You should make sure when uncoiling the rope for the first time that as you lay it out on the ground there are no repeated twists. If there are, you're uncoiling it from the wrong end. Once uncoiled, run through the new rope from one end to the other a couple of times to remove any final kinks.

◄ Using a rope bag keeps your rope clean and free from tangles

➤ If you don't uncoil your rope correctly, you can end up with knots and snags that may eventually prevent you from paying the rope out

➤ (opposite page) The stages of coiling rope

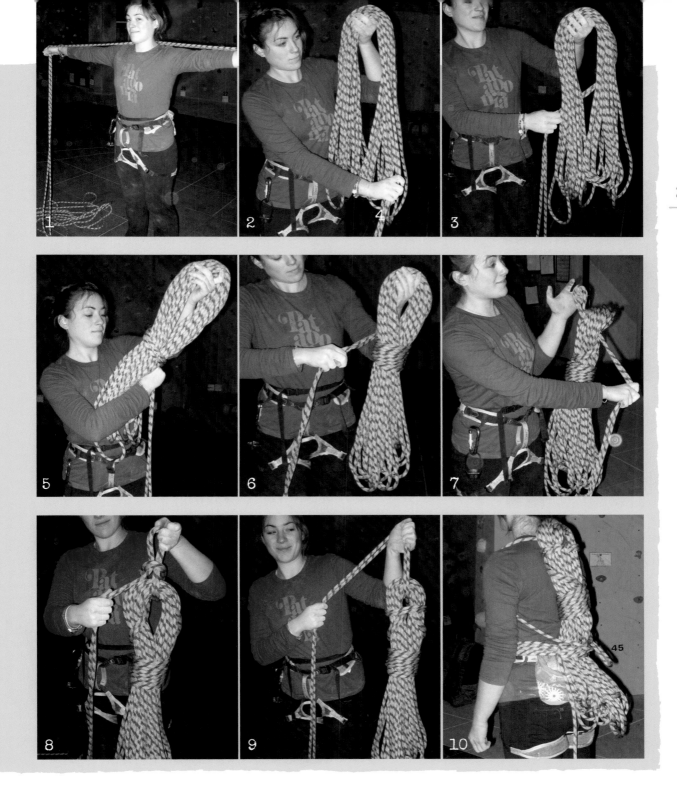

1

2

4

3

5

6

7

8

9

10

45

Quickdraws

Quickdraws provide the link between the rope and the bolt-protection systems commonly found on indoor walls. In outdoor climbing, they perform a similar function between bolts or climber-placed protection and the rope. On walls, they may be fixed in position – or you may have to provide your own.

A quickdraw is made up of two carabiners linked by a short sling. Though the length of the sling tends to be the same for indoor climbing, it might vary considerably for outdoor climbing, where it could be advantageous to extend a protection point to reduce rope drag, for example. You'll see this beneath overhangs at climbing walls.

▲ You can buy quickdraws in a range of lengths and with different carabiner configurations

Some helpful quickdraw tips

- For indoor climbing, you can count the number of bolts on the route to enable you to take the right number of quickdraws.
- For indoor climbing, short 10cm quickdraws are mostly OK.
- Your quickdraws may be easier to clip if the bottom of the carabiner is held tight to the sling by one of the small rubber insets, sometimes provided on purchase, but also available separately.

Carabiners

The carabiners on quickdraws have either solid gates or wire gates.

SOLID GATE

The solid-gate carabiners are available as a straight or bent gate. Most climbers use a straight gate to clip onto the bolt and a bent gate for the clipping the rope to. This makes sure you always clip the same carabiner into the bolt, protecting your rope against possible wear from the burrs of metal you will get from the metal-to-metal contact. The bent gate also makes clipping the rope into the carabiner a little easier. A typical weight would be between 45g and 50g.

WIRE GATE

More recently, wire-gate carabiners have become popular. They weigh less than solid bar carabiners, are more resistant to freezing up in winter if you are climbing outdoors and are less prone to opening accidentally, as a result of 'Gate-lash' (*see section on 'Why do carabiner gates open?' below*). A typical weight would be between 30g and 40g.

CHOOSING A CARABINER

The selection of carabiner is important, particularly in relation to weight and to the breaking strength when the gate is open. If you are doing a long indoor/sport climb, you may have to take between

◄▲ Solid-gate carabiners: bent and straight gate

◄ Wire-gate carabiners

10 and 20 quickdraws, making a total of between 20 and 40 carabiners. While a few grams' difference between two carabiners may not sound like much, if you multiply it by 40 it becomes significant. If you take a 50g solid-gate carabiner and compare it to a 32g wire gate, the difference in weight of 18g multiplied by 40 is 720g – a significant weight saving when you're climbing at your limit.

STRENGTH

A carabiner's strength is marked on it in three ways – each providing an illustration of breaking strength, depending on how the carabiner is loaded. The breaking strength is measured in kilonewtons (kN).

First is the standard maximum-breaking strength, when the carabiner is loaded end-to-end in each corner, next to the straightbar or 'spine'. An arrow running parallel to the direction of pull signifies this. The breaking strength is often around 24kN. The carabiner is designed to be loaded this way, so the breaking strength is at its highest. You'll see that some carabiners have a recommended rope diameter, for example, 8.5mm. This is due to the design of the specific points on the carabiner at which it is intended to be loaded. Some very specialist ultra-light carabiners designed for high-altitude use have a 20kN breaking strength, but for sport climbing 24kN and above is the norm.

You'll also see a figure for cross-loading, indicated by an arrow at right angles to the first one, showing a loading across the carabiner from side to side. This is frequently in the region of between 7kN and 8kN. It is unlikely that your carabiner will get loaded in this direction.

Finally, the breaking strength when the gate of the carabiner is open is provided – signified by a mini-engraving of a carabiner with an open gate. This figure is usually between 8kN and 10kN.

WHY DO CARABINER GATES OPEN?

How is it possible for the gate of a carabiner hanging on a vertical wall to open in the event of a fall? Take a carabiner and hold it at the base at its narrowest end. Bang the spine of the carabiner against the palm of your hand and listen. You'll hear a slight bang. This is because as the carabiner stops when it hits your hand, the momentum generated by moving it causes the gate to open slightly. The harder you hit the carabiner against your hand, the more the gate opens. It's only a momentary effect, but should a carabiner bang against the wall, or natural rock – opening the gate slightly – at the same time that it is loaded, the gate-open strength rather than the full-breaking strength may apply, and as we have seen above, there is a big difference. The carabiner can even vibrate during the loading of a fall, causing momentary gate-opening. Some people call this type of accidental opening 'Gate-lash'.

In outdoor climbing you can find other ways in which gates can open in the event of a fall, particularly where the carabiner gate is pushed against an uneven-shaped piece of rock during a fall. Gate-open strengths of 9kN and above are recommended.

Helmets

Only a very small percentage of adults wear helmets at climbing walls. Most of the time they are generally not considered necessary – for example, when bouldering or top roping. There are certain situations in which a helmet is advisable. These include lead climbing, where the nature of the moves means that a fall in an unusual angle is possible, potentially leading to falling upside down or sideways, and lead climbs where there is another section of wall at an angle to the one you are climbing on, and into which you could swing in the event of a fall.

Foam helmets are probably the most suited to indoor climbing. Normally made from expanded polystyrene with a very thin polycarbonate shell, they are light, well-ventilated and comfortable. They provide protection close to the rim, which other designs such as the hard shell tend not to do. The thicker the foam is towards the rim, the greater the level of protection provided to the climber. This feature makes this type of helmet a good choice for indoor climbing, where the main risk is banging your head against the wall in a fall.

EQUIPMENT FOR CHILDREN

Children will require all the equipment mentioned in the above sections, with the following amendments. First, a full-body harness is often used rather than a waist harness. Second, helmets are used much more commonly by children on climbing walls – and that is to be encouraged.

▾ A child in full-body harness and lightweight helmet

TAKING CARE OF YOUR EQUIPMENT

Rock shoes

The soles will accumulate dirt over time, especially if you climb outside. This reduces the level of friction and will make a noticeable difference on sloping friction holds.

To clean the soles of your rock shoes, simply use a small, bristled brush – a nail brush is ideal – and some warm water. A gentle scrub will remove all the dirt and when they are dry, you'll notice immediately how much friction has been regained when you use them. The uppers can be cleaned by brushing and by wiping with a damp cloth.

Harness

Keep your harness clean and free from dirt and chalk by brushing it regularly with a soft brush, and use a wet cloth to remove any more stubborn dirt. Harnesses are tough and will last well, but keeping them dirt-free reduces the amount of abrasion they are exposed to from tiny particles. Inspect your harness frequently and check for any obvious signs of damage. Though highly unlikely, check for any cuts or excessive abrasion in the waist belt or on the belay loop, evidence of which could mean you have to retire the harness and purchase a new one. Take a look at the instructions that come with the product and check the manufacturer's website.

Belay device

Standard belay devices without moving parts require no maintenance apart from a quick clean when dirty. Damage is normally caused by dirty ropes running through the device and acting as an abrasive agent wearing the metal and creating sharp edges. You should check your belay plate frequently for signs of wear, especially when climbing outside. Even very small amounts of wear (around 1mm) are viewed by the manufacturer as being significant enough to warrant retirement, so once again, check the instructions and manufacturer's website for full information.

Other belay devices such as the Grigri may require more specific inspection and maintenance – consult the technical details included at purchase and also consult the manufacturers' websites – companies such as Petzl provide lots of really useful information.

Carabiners

Carabiners do get dirty, and the gate-spring action can become less effective as a result. You should use a small brush and warm water to remove dirt and, periodically, you should use a tiny amount of machine oil for lubricating the gates. Wipe away any excessive oil immediately, though.

Ropes

Looking after your rope is a really important part of your climbing preparation and it's surprising how many people simply don't bother. Rope damage is generally caused by one of the following:

- Gradual wear to the sheath and core by abrasion from micro particles.
- Lowering of strength by exposure to UV light.
- Fast descents resulting in friction burns on the rope.
- Falls involving ropes running or sliding over sharper edges.
- Abseils in which tensioned ropes run or slide over sharp or abrasive edges.
- Exposure to chemicals or other degrading agents.

▼ Rope damage

To avoid rope damage you should consider the following:

- Do not walk on the ropes – this can lead to micro-particles being ground into the rope.
- Tie into opposite ends of the rope on each climb to help avoid creating twists and even wear.
- Don't abseil or lower too fast as this produces friction, the heat from which can damage a rope. Abseil devices can get hot enough to melt rope.
- Use a rope bag both indoors and outdoors to protect your rope from dirt.
- Keep your rope away from contact with sharp objects or contaminants.
- Don't leave in a place exposed to sunlight.

Keep your ropes clean. Dirty ropes wear out carabiners and belay plates. Washing ropes in warm water is recommended, and you can make or buy a bristled tube to pull your rope through while washing to really get rid of the dirt.

How long should my equipment last?

Check the manufacturers' information carefully, but generally 10 years is the maximum life for most equipment. Please note it can be much lower than this depending on the type and level of use (*see above*). In any case, equipment should be replaced after a major fall or loading. Don't use equipment whose history is unknown (second-hand equipment, for example) and if you're not sure, simply bin it! Many climbing walls have a 'BMC bin' especially for this purpose – the gear is recycled by greenpeakgear.co.uk, with proceeds going to the British Mountaineering Council access and conservation trust.

Buying second-hand climbing equipment

Don't! You don't know what it's been subjected to and how old it is. The exceptions may be rock shoes, chalk bags and clothing.

FINDING
A
WALL

Perhaps you've never tried climbing before, or maybe you've had a go at school or on an activity holiday and want to do more. Maybe you want to use climbing as a way of getting fit and you want to try your hand at indoor climbing. So, how do you make a start?

FINDING A WALL AND YOUR FIRST VISIT

The first place to look is the internet. Search for climbing walls in your area or look at the British Mountaineering Council's Directory of Climbing Walls (www.thebmc.co.uk). Most climbing walls have good websites with details of opening hours, admission prices, rules, regulations, and so on.

Once you've found a wall to visit, your choices are simple. If you're lucky enough to have friends who are already experienced climbers, you may be able to persuade them to sign you in at the wall under their supervision and get them to show you the basics. If you don't have climbing friends, contact your local wall and find out what it can offer you as a beginner.

Due to the potential hazards involved in climbing indoors, all centres will offer some sort of induction system for non-climbers – or climbers with limited experience – before they can climb unsupervised. This is to ensure that everyone has the sufficient skills and understanding to climb without endangering either themselves or other wall users.

Adults (over 18)

Each climbing wall will have its own range of courses and induction methods, often including ones for beginner adults. They include:

- Taster sessions – have a go and see if you enjoy it.
- Private instruction – pay by the hour.
- Group instruction – you can have fun, fall off and laugh at each other.

▲ Signing in at Kendal Wall reception

▲ Getting a small group of friends together for instruction is a great idea

▲ It's important to learn crucial skills such as belaying, while putting your jacket on

RULES AND REGULATIONS

All climbing walls will have a set of rules and regulations. When you sign in at any wall you will need to agree that you will abide by their rules.

Risks

All climbing walls have a participation statement that includes something to the effect that the British Mountaineering Council recognises that climbing and mountaineering are activities with a danger of personal injury or death. You must make your own assessment of the risks whenever you climb.

Unsupervised climbing

Before you climb without supervision, climbing walls will expect you to be able to use a safety harness, know appropriate knots to attach a rope to the harness and a belay device to secure a falling climber using a rope. You will have to register and state that you know how to use the equipment, will abide by the rules and understand the risks.

Novices will not be allowed to climb without supervision. Typically, wall staff will ask a series of questions to determine your knowledge and experience and if they are in doubt may ask you to complete a short practical test prior to allowing you to climb unsupervised. Some walls have a mandatory test in place regardless of your experience.

To learn climbing skills, you could try one of the following:

Bouldering induction The simplest way to get into climbing on your own to start with.

Beginners' scheme (Boulderer/Top roper/Lead climber/Complete climber) This local scheme consists of four levels of training and competence.

NICAS scheme A comprehensive scheme to acquire personal skills and develop as an indoor climber, right through to competition level.

Climb with friends If you have friends who are experienced climbers, you could learn the basic skills from them. They will need to be registered as experienced adult climbers and they will need to sign to agree to be responsible for you.

Under 18s

If you're under 18, there are different rules relating to supervision and you'll need to go along to the wall with a parent or guardian initially. The Association of British Climbing Walls recommends a minimum age of 14 for unsupervised climbing, following a thorough assessment of both your competence and your risk awareness. Depending on your age, you'll find a range of kid's clubs and sessions.

Children

It's normal that children must be supervised by an adult whilst at the centre unless they have been assessed and registered for unsupervised climbing by the management. It's easy for unsupervised children to get a bit carried away. You need to be certain they have the maturity to co-exist happily with older climbers and to climb safely.

General safety

Most centres will expect you to do the following:

- Report to reception before you climb.
- Take care, use common sense and look out for your personal safety at all times.
- Report any problems with walls, equipment or other climbers' behaviour to members of staff immediately: for example, loose holds or someone climbing in an unsafe manner.
- Be aware of how your actions will affect other climbers.
- Never distract people while they are climbing or belaying.
- Do not stand underneath someone else who is climbing unless you are belaying or spotting.

Specific equipment The notes below are taken from Kendal Wall's regulations regarding specific equipment and will be similar to those at most walls. The notes in italics are the author's.

TALL WALLS

When climbing:

- Tall walls are designed to be climbed using a rope for protection. Solo climbing is not acceptable and climbers should always use a rope to protect themselves on these climbs.
- Always use a safety harness to attach yourself to the rope.
- Always tie the rope directly into the harness using a figure-of-eight knot.

BELAYING

- Always use a belay device correctly attached to your safety harness. 'Traditional' or 'body' belaying is not acceptable.
- The attachment points on the floor and the sandbags are provided to give support to people belaying a climber who is much heavier than they are. Direct belays from these points or sandbags are not acceptable. *Direct belaying is when you attach a belay device directly to an anchor point rather than your harness.*
- Always stand when belaying. Sitting or lying is not acceptable whilst belaying at floor level.
- Always stand as close to the climbing wall as is practical.

TOP ROPING

- Some of the climbs in the centre have top ropes already in place. Please leave them in place when you have finished with them. Do not take them down to use on other routes. Do not put your rope into the same lower-off point as a top rope.

LEADING

- When using the lead walls you must supply your own appropriately rated dynamic rope. Do not use the centre's top ropes for lead climbing.
- *Some centre rope are semi-static and don't absorb shock like a normal lead climbing rope.*
- Running belay attachments (quickdraws) are provided on some BUT NOT ALL of the lead walls.
- Ensure you have sufficient quickdraws for the route you plan to lead. You must clip all the quickdraws or bolts on the route you are climbing. *Make sure you count the number of quickdraws required and take enough with you.*

BOULDERING

- Always climb within your capabilities and descend by down climbing as far as possible or at least by a controlled fall. *Don't make a habit of getting to the top of the wall and jumping off. You could injure yourself and it kicks up a lot of dust.*
- Never climb directly above or below another climber.
- Never leave any gear on the boulder mats.

▲ Someone's gone mad with the paintbrush! The Pinnacle, Northampton – a cheery new wall built in a modern industrial unit

➤ Inside The Castle climbing wall. Indoor climbing with character

INSIDE THE WALL

As a non-climber, your first visit to a climbing wall may be intimidating. The leading walls may look very big and steep, and bouldering areas even steeper.

Layout

Indoor climbing walls are very varied in layout and type. The walls themselves will be made up of different colours and textures, while the buildings housing them range from modern industrial units and old churches to disused squash courts and old factories. Just like outdoor crags, each wall has its own character.

Some walls specialise solely in bouldering, and have no roped areas. Others provide a mix of roped climbing and bouldering. Many have dedicated training areas and some have gyms, physiotherapists and climbing shops. They may share space with other companies, for example, those training people in roped access or even facilities such as skate parks.

One of the first things you should do is to get acquainted with everything your local climbing walls have to offer and give them a try – you'll probably find that you prefer certain walls to others.

Bouldering areas

Bouldering involves challenging yourself on short climbs and traverses on which no rope is needed. The 'problem' areas are protected by thick matting to make them safer, although this does not automatically guarantee an injury-free climb. Bouldering areas are great fun and provide excellent training, as well as offering a perfect opportunity to climb if you're on your own. Some indoor climbers only use bouldering areas, and never go on the roped climbs; some use bouldering

as a way of keeping fit. Others enjoy the competitive side of this type of climbing and may enter local or national competitions. Most walls change boulder configurations regularly and provide a graded list of problems for you to try. Some walls have several bouldering areas.

Dedicated training areas

You'll find some walls are better equipped for training than others. In some, the facilities may be in an open part of the wall for everyone to use; in others, they may be in a dedicated training room. Some walls insist you have an induction before using the training facilities; others may have an age limit for entry. This is due to concerns that some training methods may not be safe for growing children. Training facilities include campus rungs, fingerboards, pull-up holds and boards, systems board, weight-training facilities, warm-up equipment (for example, exercise bikes) and dry tooling training.

Some climbing walls have gyms and you may have to pay extra to use them and undergo an induction session.

▾ A typical modern bouldering area in Milton Keynes, Buckinghamshire

▲ A dedicated training room at Kendal Wall

▲ Dry-tool training area at Northampton

▲ Open-plan training area at The Arch

With the increasingly competitive nature of indoor climbing and the potential for future inclusion as an Olympic sport, training facilities, training methods and access to coaching are all likely to undergo significant future changes.

Top rope and lead climbing areas

The biggest – sometimes extremely impressive – sections of indoor walls are for roped climbing. Some climbs are set up with top ropes already in

▲ Lots of top roping at Reading Wall. You can easily see the 'lower-off points' at the top of each climb

▲ Systems Board at Redpoint, Birmingham

Roped climbing areas vary in height and steepness and may have several different angle changes in the course of one route.

Climbing shops

Climbing shops are quite commonly found at indoor walls, so you can check out some bargains and the latest gear before or after you climb.

▲ Campus, pull-up and fingerboard training facilities at Kendal Wall

➤ A busy leading session at Kendal Wall

place, some are equipped with quickdraws for lead climbing; others may be equipped only with bolts, leaving the lead climber to attach his or her own quickdraws. All roped climbs have a 'lower off' at the top of the climb – usually consisting of two linked anchor points with a double carabiner. The lower off is already clipped on climbs set up for top roping, but lead climbers clip their rope into this point to be lowered back down. The wall staff will change the climbs periodically and may change the sections that have top ropes fixed and those available for leading.

TERMINOLOGY

It's as well at this point to start to get to grips with the terminology found in climbing walls, and firstly relating to the walls themselves.

Features of the wall

Looking around the wall you'll probably have noticed that the climbs tackle lots of different angles and features. Climbing walls are varied and offer a range of different types of climbing through the steepness and design of the wall features.

You may notice that while some sections are designed to resemble natural rock, some parts of the wall are much more abstract and brightly coloured – a bit like a giant adventure playground. Climbing walls are carefully designed to incorporate many different features and to offer a wide variety of styles of climbing. A great deal of thought goes into building them and the designs can be enormously complex. Most climbing walls will offer a similar range of features. The following section lists some of key features.

WALL ANGLES

Vertical Speaks for itself – 90 degrees to the ground.
Off vertical A term used to describe walls that are close to, but at slightly easier angles than vertical – you'll be glad of angles like this to give your arms a rest.
Slab angle Slabs are generally 70 degrees and under.
Overhanging At a greater angle than vertical but varying in steepness. Usually used in conjunction with a description, for example, slightly overhanging. (Note the difference to 'overhang', described below in the *Key features* section.)

KEY FEATURES

Overlaps Can be found on walls of varying angles and are basically small overhangs.
Overhangs A significant obstacle where the wall above bulges out sharply – usually at about 90 degrees, smaller than a **Roof**.
Roof A sizeable horizontal feature, bigger than an overhang; it can be quite intimidating as well as strenuous.
Bulges A rounded overhang.

Top roping

Corner groove

Lower offs

Bulge

Quickdraw

Resting on the lead

Corner

Small overhang

Overhanging wall

Slab

Vertical wall with features and bolt ons

Arete

Corner with corner crack

Route grade signs

Belayer

Overhanging Arete

Overhanging wall

Arete

Corner

Bulge

Volume

Slab

Stepped overhang

Overlap

The BMC Leading Ladder		2012 - 2013

Grade **7b** 20

Feet REC

Hands RED

Comments NO BRIDGING

BMC **Route Label**

Colour	Grade	Description	Setter	Date
PURPLE/GREEN SPOTS	6a+		Charlie	Aug 2012
FLURO YELLOW	6b		Charlie	Sep 2012
RED	7b	NO BRIDGING	StefMac	Oct 2012

ALL ROUTES ON LINES 17.5 TO 28 INCLUDE ALL FEATURES, ARETE S, BRIDGING, CRACKS ETC UNLESS STATED NO DISCS.
FEEDBACK?
nowaythats5a@castle-climbing.co.uk

20 castle climbing centre

▲ At the bottom of each climbing section, you'll find a small sign with route grades linked to the colours of the holds

Lip The term used to describe the edge of an overhang.

Corner Two surfaces facing each other like the pages in an open book. The angle can vary from a shallow corner (more open book) to a deeper one (more closed book).

Arêtes The opposite to a corner, like the outside edge of an open book, often vertical or overhanging, usually has quite sharp features.

Grooves A groove is essentially a shallow and less-defined corner (see **Corner**, above).

Cracks These are usually too small to get the body into and vary from finger to shoulder width, for example:

- *Finger crack* – Finger width.
- *Hand jamming crack* – Wide enough to put your hand in.
- *Off-width crack* – Knee and shoulder width.

Chimney Big enough fissure to get your body into.

Bolt-ons The colour-coded hand- and footholds that are bolted to the walls to create routes.

Volumes Large, moveable shapes that attach to the main wall to provide variety. They may have moulded or bolt-on holds, or both.

Features Moulded sections of walls have more natural-looking features built in to them, including edges, pockets and cracks, making the climbing feel more like outdoor rock.

Some of these terms are used in conjunction with each other to give a more accurate description, for example an 'overhanging corner' or a 'vertical crack'.

Other wall terminology

Lower offs The points at the top of the wall from which climbers are lowered back down, usually consisting of two bolts linked to a single point, sometimes called a 'Y hang'.

Bolts The small, but very strong attachments that the quickdraws clip into.

Route info At the foot of each wall section, a route card will tell you what routes have been set, matching colours with grades. It's worth noting that the colours of the bolt-on holds are not graded like ski runs or mountain bike trails for example.

You should by now know your way around a wall, be able to tell a quickdraw from a lower off and a chimney from an off-width. So, it's time to get onto the serious stuff and take a closer look at the climbing wall and give you some basic climbing knowledge and techniques.

4

STARTING TO CLIMB

You're standing looking up at the huge roped wall with your instructor. A woman with a red top is climbing very gently and gracefully in one section on a vertical wall, making it all look so easy. You're thinking that you might stand a chance on that one.

On the overhanging wall, a brute of a climber is snatching from hold to hold, his feet flying off the footholds as he forces his way to the top. You're impressed: it's steep and there's so much effort going into it – it must be really hard. You decide you'll keep away from that one for a while.

Your instructor explains the grades to you and you discover that the climb being dispatched so effortlessly by the lady is in fact several grades harder than the overhanging wall that was attacked so fiercely and seemingly impressively by the man.

'It's all down to technique,' your instructor says. 'Come and take another look.'

You go back to watching the woman in the red top and take a closer look. Actually, the holds she's using are very small and some of them are a long way apart. She is placing her feet gently and precisely on the holds and she reminds you of a ballet dancer. The handholds she uses are caressed to feel for the perfect place to grip before her fingers lock tightly in position. She makes it look so easy. You check out the man again. His movements are jerky, verging on uncontrolled. His feet are

◄ Pure strength isn't everything – although it does help!

▲ Bridging makes a difficult position seem easier and more relaxed

slapped onto the footholds and sometimes slip off. He grasps at the handholds, often adjusting the position of his hands once he has hold of them.

You're still looking up at the woman in the red top as your instructor talks you through the climbs and starts to discuss balance and control, flexibility and technique. You now know which climbing style you want to copy.

To understand good technique, you need to know the names of the hand and footholds, as well as all the basic techniques of movement on the wall. You also need to know how to use the holds to best effect.

HANDHOLDS AND FOOTHOLDS

Looking at the wall more closely you'll see many different-shaped and -sized holds – most of them bolted to the wall, but some incorporated as moulded features. You might also see cracks running in different directions. You'll hear climbers using lots of varied terminology to describe handholds of different shapes and sizes. Some of these terms are, and have been, in widespread use; others are more regional and may make little sense to you to start with.

Handholds

A 'jug' is a large hold – a 'massive jug' (sometimes called a 'bucket') an even bigger one!

An 'edge' is just as it sounds – like the edge of a brick and may be used in conjunction with other adjectives in order for the speaker to be more precise – for

▲ 'Jugs'

▽ A 'jug'

example, 'small edge', 'sharp edge', 'sloping edge'.

'Small edges' may also be called 'crimps', 'grattons' or 'super grattons' – the latter two originate from the Fontainebleau boulders. These types of hold are small – usually between the width of the edge of a beer mat and the width of a finger.

An 'incut' hold is one where the gripping surface is turned in towards the rock at an angle of greater than 90 degrees. The more incut the hold is, the more you can pull outwards on it, as well as downwards.

A 'positive' hold is generally one that is at about 90 degrees to the wall. It might also be called a flat.

◂ Fingers crammed onto a 'small', but 'positive' edge

⌃ A shallow pocket hold, using the thumb to create a pinch grip

⌃ A positive hold doesn't have to be big

A 'pocket' is usually a hole in the rock into which you can cram as many fingers as possible for maximum grip. They are very common on limestone. 'Tiny pockets' into which you can get just one finger into are called 'monos'.

A 'sidepull' is a hold you use sideways and is sometimes also called a 'layaway'. When you're climbing on real rock, this is a very common hold.

An 'undercut' is a hold you use by holding it palm up and pulling outwards and upwards.

⌃ An open hand position on this pocket hold

➤ Using a sidepull

▲ Using an undercut hold on Bosworth Academy's King Kong training wall   ⌄ A pinch grip

▲ Nick Moulden holding a sloper

A 'pinch grip' is used on a hold where you grip between fingers and thumb – it is very common on outdoor climbing as well.

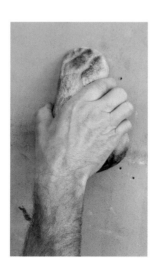

A 'sloper' is a sloping handhold, the type that demands precision and strong hands to be used effectively.

Sometimes these terms are used in conjunction with each other to describe a particular hold – a good example would be an 'undercut pocket', indicating a hole-shaped handhold that you can pull upwards and outwards on.

Cracks

Cracks in the rock face have their own set of terminology, often related to the width of the crack – here are the basic terms, but the techniques are dealt with in the Advanced Techniques section in Chapter 7.

Thin, vertically orientated cracks that can take the tips of your fingers through to base of finger width are called 'finger cracks', on which you use a 'finger jam'.

▲ A finger crack

Wider cracks than this enable you to fit all or part of your hand in – this is called the classic 'hand jam'.

Slightly wider cracks take 'fist jams' (which are uncommon on indoor walls); while still wider cracks, called 'off widths', start to require the jamming of arms and shoulders, and the use of 'arm bars', where your hand is flat on one side and your upper arm flat on the other. Fortunately, these strength-sapping cracks are few and far between at indoor walls!

Even wider cracks become 'chimneys' and require 'chimneying' techniques such as 'back and footing'.

▲ Ascending a chimney at The Pinnacle Climbing Wall, Northampton, using the classic back and foot technique: progress is made by shunting your back up the wall and swapping feet

Footholds

Most holds on climbing walls protrude from the wall, though on some of the designs which aim to provide a more natural feel to the climbing you'll find inset holds and pockets that don't protrude. There tend to be a smaller number of terms for footholds than for handholds, which is simply because your fingers can achieve more variety of grip than your foot can, encased in a tight rock shoe.

An 'edge' is the same as for handholds.

◄ Hand jam

⌄ Smearing involves placing the foot on a sloping hold to maximise friction

⌄ Smearing in a corner

⌃ A large foothold

⌄ A small edge used as a foothold

'Smearing' involves using a hold or more likely a whole rock surface set at an angle and can be used by simply frictioning the feet onto it, using any slight variations in angle or shape to help you grip.

You can also use a similar friction technique to tackle a corner or angle in the rock. Imagine a right-angled corner – placing your toe right into the angle will provide friction between the toe and the corner and between each side of your rock shoe and each wall side. This can feel quite positive.

The terms 'big foothold', 'small foothold' and 'sloping foothold' are self-explanatory.

A 'crease' may be used for hands or feet, and is a slight linear indentation in the wall that may be at any angle.

'Toe jams' are found where the vertical crack is just wide enough to let the toe of your boot in, but not your foot. On wider cracks you may get 'foot

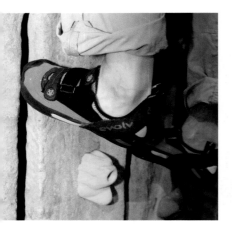

▾ ➤ Two examples of using cracks as footholds

jams', where the whole foot can enter the crack.

On still wider cracks, you start to use a range of 'off-width' (between crack and chimney width) techniques such as a 'knee lock' (see page 101) and 'chimneying' (wide enough to get into) techniques.

USING HAND AND FOOTHOLDS CORRECTLY

Good climbers make climbing look easy. A leading climber like Dave Birkett will demonstrate the same precision and care on a grade 4 climb as he would on a 7a. Everything he does is measured, in control, and very precise. A friend and I were once bouldering on Dartmoor with Dave and were roundly beaten on a problem, even though Dave had paused to light a cigarette halfway through the hard bit!

As a newcomer to climbing, you should strive to emulate leading climbers by climbing every route you try out in as controlled and precise a manner as they would. It won't work all the time, of course. For example, there may be occasions when you panic as your arms tire and you may snatch for

▾ Good climbers make it look so easy!

holds and tap your rock shoe up the wall until it lands awkwardly on a hold where it starts shaking uncontrollably and it spreads up your leg until you look like Elvis – and fall back onto the rope!

Even as a beginner, you can look and climb better by understanding and practising some basic skills. These will hold you in good stead throughout your climbing career, providing core technique that you can build on as you climb more and climb

◄ Especially at greater heights you have to be able to rely on your grip

▲ Chalking up ready for some steep moves

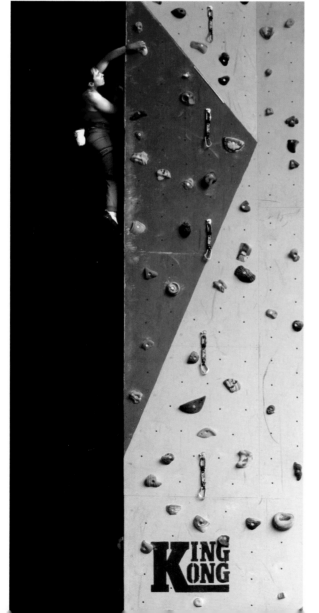

harder. It can take months or even years to hone the more advanced techniques, though.

This section will help you understand how to use the holds described and named in the previous section.

Using handholds correctly

Chalk up! The use of chalk improves the friction between your hand and the holds and dries off any moisture. Holds can become too heavily chalked and require a brush off – it's your hands that need the chalk, not the hold.

▲ Use your fingers together for collective strength

Most beginners reach for a handhold, grasp it and pull on it. A handhold is seen as something to be pulled down on – after all if you want to move up you need to pull down ... don't you?

First and foremost, you need to make the handhold work for you. It may be used to move you in any direction through 360 degrees, so simply grabbing hold of it is not enough. Think back to the woman in the red top. You watched her and she caressed the holds, before she locked onto them.

Each time you reach for a handhold, let your fingers explore it until you find precisely the best place to grip – even on a 'jug', though this mightn't be possible when making dynamic moves. It's not a complex or time-consuming process – the best way to develop this skill is to walk around the climbing wall and, either looking away or closing your eyes, let your fingers explore the hold until they settle onto the ideal place. We're talking millimetre precision here. Try this on a dozen or so holds of different sizes and shapes and you'll begin to get the idea. While climbing, try and put this into practice on as many handholds as possible, no matter the size. On harder climbs, it can be the difference between hanging on and falling off.

Using a hold to its best advantage usually involves having all four fingers close together, but on some more complex holds, you'll find it easier to separate your fingers to some extent. If you do this, beware of placing too much strain on certain fingers as it may cause injury – your fingers are at their strongest when used collectively, close together and at the same angle.

On most handholds, but particularly smaller ones, your thumb is much more important than you might at first think. On small holds (edges, super grattons and so on), use your thumb by pushing it against your forefinger and against the hold. You may also place your thumb over the top of your forefinger, especially on the smallest crimps.

To lock onto small edges, use the process already mentioned to settle your fingers into exactly the right place on the hold, then put your wrist in towards the wall and pull down so your middle knuckle sticks up. Place your thumb either

▼ Feel how the thumb increases grip power by overlapping the forefinger

◄ A more open grip on a positive hold

➤ Will Birkett using two pocket holds. You can see how it would be possible to pull on them at different angles other than straight down

against or on top of your forefinger, lock your fingers and start pulling! It's worth remembering that using a small crimp is one of the main causes of finger injury, so be gentle to start with and try and use a more open-handed technique. These will be covered later in this chapter.

When using a 'positive' hold, you'll often use your thumb on the hold edge or pressed against your forefinger to give maximum grip, but once again, feel around to get the best position before you lock on. On some positive holds, you'll use a more open grip, without crimping.

'Pockets' come in all sorts of shapes and sizes and especially when incut they hold your fingers together and feel really good. On larger pocket holds, you'll need to take care to place your fingers in the best position and often you can put your fingers to one side of the pocket and use it to lean sideways off as well as pull down on. This can improve the distance you can reach for the next hold. Sometimes you can also turn them into undercut holds as you move up.

On smaller pocket holds, you may have to experiment with cramming different fingers into the pocket until you achieve the most powerful grip possible. Once again, you may find you can turn a downward pull into a sideways one in order to increase the distance you can reach.

Most people naturally pull down on holds, but the truth is that many handholds are used at different angles – such as sidepulls and undercuts.

The layout of the footholds and the distance to, and position of, the next handhold dictate the direction in which you pull on a hold. One of the secrets of using handholds is understanding that pulling sideways or underneath on an appropriate handhold can significantly increase the distance you can reach to gain your next handhold.

You may also find that you commence a move by using the hold in a downwards direction, but as you gain height and rearrange your feet on new

◀ Using a hold as a sidepull – note the body position to the side of the hold.

▶ You can reach a long way from an undercut hold

footholds, you swivel your hand around so that it pulls on the hold in a different direction to enable you to complete the move. Using handholds in this way is something you'll need to experiment with

and it's worth spending time on it, as it is a valuable skill.

Don't forget to experiment with your foot and body positions at the same time though – for example, the further beneath a sidepull you are, or the lower you are in relation to an undercut, the less use it will be. Conversely, the more you move sideways in relation to a sidepull, and the higher you are in relation to an undercut, the better they will feel. The same principles about careful placement of the fingers still apply.

The 'pinchgrip' is a very useful type of hold. The fact that you're using this technique is indicative that the hold does not have a positive edge you can pull down on. You therefore hold it between your thumb and fingers, tensing your hand to get the maximum grip. Depending on the size of the hold, your fingers may be stretched out or folded in, in which case you should use the edge of your folded forefinger to grip the hold. Try some pinchgrips out and see what you can hang on to. You'll notice that if you move to the side of a pinchgrip, you start to turn it into a sidepull, thereby combining two techniques. Pinchgripping is very common. The

▲ Moving from down-pull to undercut

◄ Bill Birkett pinchgripping up a vertical feature

▼ Holding a 'sloper' requires strong hands and forearms

hardest ones to hold onto are the largest, most rounded holds. You'll need good hand and finger strength to use these effectively. 'Slopers' are another difficult hold. Once again you need to place your hand with precision on a sloper, finding the exact place at which the grip feels best. You might use your thumb to combine a pinch grip or you may simply place it to the side of your fingers and friction it to get even more grip.

To use a sloping hold you need to introduce

some hand tension. To do this, you have to force your fingers onto the slope of the hold – you should be able to feel the tension running right back to your shoulder. To try this out, place your hand on a flat surface – a tabletop is ideal – and experiment with hand tension, wrist and arm position to get the maximum possible grip when pulling across the surface. Slopers are found extensively in outdoor climbing, especially on gritstone.

Crack climbing is an essential skill for the outdoor climber, but perhaps less so for the indoor climber. Crack climbing technique are dealt with in Chapter 7.

Stand easy – using footholds

For an experienced, high-standard climber, a tiny variation in rock angle, pebble or beer mat edge-sized dimple constitutes a foothold. By comparison, the sort of foothold you visualise when you start climbing would be akin to an overnight bivouac ledge to them.

▲ This large foothold would seem small to most beginners

As you become more experienced, you'll use smaller and smaller holds and your technical ability to use them will increase. What you thought of as tiny footholds will become decent ones, and you'll be able to use holds that you would not even have been aware of when you first started climbing.

Footholds vary in four main ways – friction, useable surface area, front-on angle and sideways slope.

Let's go back to the two climbers we watched on our first visit as described at the opening of the chapter. The woman in the red top – you watched her place her feet with amazing precision, while the 'jug thug' simply planted his feet anywhere, almost kicking the holds into submission in the process. Using footholds is about precision – *absolute* precision.

Watch a really good climber work with small footholds – they will, whenever possible, lean away from the wall slightly to allow themselves to look carefully at the foothold. They will then gently place their foot on the hold – often with the heel a little down and perhaps move it slightly and feel it onto the very best place, rather like using handholds as

▾ Careful foot placement is essential; it helps to lean slightly back and look down

described above. They will then lift their heel up slightly and, tensing the foot and lower leg muscles transfer their weight to the hold.

At this point the muscles in your feet and toes should be working hard – especially through your big toe, when using footholds in more standard positions.

We've just mentioned how there are some standard variations in footholds and it's the same with your feet – there are several specific ways you can use them – which one you use depends on the relationship between the size/shape/orientation of the foothold and the handholds you are using to make the move.

The most common position is with the foot placed at around 45 degrees to the hold, with the big toe doing most of the work. This position uses both the front and side of your rock shoe.

The further you move position so that your heel is fully away from the rock, the more of the front of your big toe you use, the more leverage you get and the harder it is to hold the position – especially on very small holds. Conversely this position allows you to take more weight on your feet and less on your hands, as the relative position of your bodyweight is altered. This is particularly useful on slabs as it allows you to easily see where the next footholds are, and puts you in good balance.

The further you move the inside of your foot and heel towards the wall, the more of the edge of your foot you will be using. This will make it feel like your upper body is being pushed away from the wall, even though it acts to keep your hips in close and get more weight through your feet – especially useful on steep sections.

Sometimes you will use the outside of your foot around the little toe area – typically when using a sidepull hold and performing twist lock moves (see Chapter 7).

The vertical angle of your foot will also vary. On comfortable, larger footholds, your heel will tend

▲ To stand out on your toes you need strong feet and calf muscles

◀ Climbers often use the outside edge of their foot in conjunction with sidepull handholds

to drop slightly into a relaxed position. It may then tense so that you stand more on your toe as you begin the next move. Relaxing your heel will also stop your foot shaking if you get the wobbles.

▲ Relaxing your heel helps stop any leg shake

The position of your heel in relation to your toe in vertical alignment will depend on a number of factors, including the level of friction, the angle of the surface of the hold and the size of the foothold. As with handholds, it is very beneficial for newcomers to climbing to experiment with foot positions and to find out what works best for different types of moves.

Ultimately, the way you use any foot or handhold will depend on its relationship with the other holds available at that point, the move below which brought you there, and the next move you make.

Big footholds are easy to stand on but you should still experiment with your foot position to find the best placement, and you should still place your foot with care.

Small edges are normally used with the foot turned more at an angle to the wall – there's simply not enough rigidity to stand comfortably with your heel away from the wall. Using small edges demands precision and you'll find tensing your big toe right through to your calf muscles will help achieve maximum stability. Overplacing your foot (see tips overleaf) will also help get the most out of these small holds.

Pocket footholds demand a greater use of the point of your toe, which in turn places more stress on your foot and calf muscles. Developing strong calf and foot muscles is highly beneficial when it

◄ Smearing on a steep slab angle at Kendal Wall

comes to using smaller footholds. You'll find yourself lowering your heel slightly and then raising it to cram the toe of your rock shoe into the pocket.

Most footholds on climbing walls stick out, but you do come across incut holds. These are most frequently dealt with with a similar technique to edging – using the inside of the big toe area and overplacing slightly to ensure you're making the most of the available hold area.

Using sloping holds or simply a sloping rock/wall surface is often called 'smearing'. A big leap forwards in outdoor climbing standards occurred in the 1980s, with the introduction of a stickier rubber on the Boreal Fire rock shoe. Suddenly, sloping rock features that had previously been unusable became friction holds and the use of smearing holds, especially on gritstone, created some magnificent climbs. Often you have to make use of tiny, almost imperceptible variations in rock or wall angle to get the most effective smears. Using the real slopers requires good technique and a lot of confidence. As with all type of holds, you need to experiment to find the limits of what is possible – never forgetting that the currently impossible might become only just impossible, a subsequent possibility and eventually quite possible!

Some helpful tips

1 Don't be surprised if you find your feet moving to different positions and different holds several times while your hands remain in the same place.

2 Get used to the idea that on protruding climbing wall holds, your foot routinely rotates on the hold as your body changes position ready for the next move.

3 Try 'overplacing' your foot on smaller holds. This means angling your foot back in relation to the hold and placing your foot on it so that as you stand up on it, it pushes a little bit against the wall surface before engaging the hold. The result is that you'll get your foot as tightly in against the wall and use the maximum amount of the foothold possible. You might even get a bit of extra friction against the wall from the rand of your rock shoe (that is, the rubber that is not on the sole) using this technique. Every little helps.

◄ ▲ Overplacing on a foothold, first tilting the foot back slightly and positioning correctly then placing the foot onto the hold, so that the toe rubber is forced tight into the wall

BASIC CLIMBING MOVES

Along with the key ways to use the most common holds, you also need to master the most common basic techniques.

Push down

This is a very useful technique, often used in conjunction with bridging, but also in many other situations. Push downs can be performed on holds, but are often associated with slabs and features. Normally, one hand (the higher) has a good hold, while the other (lower) hand pushes down in opposition to it. This type of move often creates a triangle shape between the two arms and the wall.

➤ Using a push down as part of a bridging move

Laybacking

A common technique in outdoor climbing for ascending cracks, especially in corners, laybacking may be used on crack systems on indoor walls and the technique is often used on bolt-on holds and volumes for individual moves rather than for long series of moves.

Laybacking involves opposing forces – the pull of your hands opposing the push of your feet. This could be in a corner crack, on an arête or ridge or simply using sidepulls on a flat wall.

◀ ➤ Laybacking moves

Chimneying

Chimneys are wide fissures that the climber's whole body can fit into. They are usually ascended by 'back and footing', which involves placing your back against one side of the chimney and your feet against the opposite side. Your hands push down on the wall behind your back, or you may have one hand on each side. Shuffling up a little at a time, progress is quite rapid. This technique can be easier or harder depending on the width of the chimney.

It is possible to use a chimneying position to gain a rest in other situations, such as where the rock forms a corner – it's an under-used technique on indoor walls.

◄ Resting in a chimneying position

Palming

Used commonly, but not exclusively, on slabs, palming involves pushing down (often on friction) with one hand, while the other hand pulls down on a higher hold. The palming position provides a good downwards force and also usually acts as a counter to the hand which is pulling, retaining a good, balanced position. It is similar to a push down but relies purely on friction.

▾ Palming

Bridging

This very common technique is one of the best ways to take a rest as well as aid upward progress. Bridging involves standing on footholds on opposite sides of a corner feature in such a way that it is possible to take all or most of your weight off your hands. The foot and hip position is variable and responds to the layout of the holds. Experienced climbers can bridge out on friction or small 'smears' in climbing wall corners.

▲ Bridging

Mantleshelfing

This move is not that common on indoor walls, but is used often enough to mention. Imagine climbing onto a high mantelpiece. You start by pulling up and then straightening the arms so that they take your weight. One leg is then placed on the ledge. You then stand up on this leg, usually finding a handhold to help with the standing movement. The ideal handhold is a sidepull – for example, if you put your right leg onto the ledge, you'd be looking to turn to the right and find a hold to pull sideways against with your right hand. Complete the standing movement to establish yourself on the ledge and you have completed a mantelshelf. This type of move can also be made on smaller holds than ledges.

ˇˆ Dave Birkett demonstrating a difficult mantleshelf move. Note how he uses his heel to provide a slightly easier position on this small ledge, enabling him to keep his hips closer into the rock

Rockover

Another common technique, used when there is a foothold high to one side, is the rockover. Let's say it's to the right. Your handholds are gripped tight, and your feet can either use small intermediate holds or friction up the wall until you can get your right foot on the high hold. Keeping your hands on the same holds, you then 'rock' your weight over onto the foothold, keeping your hips close to the wall, so that you can push up with your leg, aided by your hands. Once partially or sometimes fully stood up, you then reposition your hands and complete the move. Don't be tempted to reach up too soon – make sure your hip and weight is right over your top foothold, creating a stable position before you reach for the next hold.

BALANCE AND POSITION

I remember many years ago trying out boulder problems near Chamonix with some local French climbers. One particularly awkward problem defeated me completely and it was with some embarrassment that I watched the ease with which one of the local lads climbed it. After stepping gently to the ground at the end of the traverse, he looked across at me and just said, '*C'est un question d'equilibre!*' I thought it was perhaps also a question of finger strength, power and flexibility!

Good balance and positional know-how is so important. Some people have a head start, if they have a great sense of balance and naturally adopt good positions. Others, like me, have to learn how to do it, which takes time and effort.

⌄ A rockover – a series showing getting the high foothold, then rocking bodyweight forwards and upwards, leaving the hands on the same holds before finally making a long reach for the next hold.

Being balanced and adopting good positions benefits the climber in several ways. First, it reduces the amount of strength and energy expenditure needed to stay in any given position. Second, it has a valuable psychological benefit – helping to keep you calm and in control. Third, it makes subsequent moves easier as you are in the correct position to make them; and fourth, you just look good!

To achieve the best balance and positions in climbing you must try to visualise your centre of gravity.

If you're standing straight up in a normal position, your centre of gravity runs down the centre of your body. You don't have to do much to remain in balance as your feet form a stable platform for gravity to pull against.

If you then lean to one side, your centre of gravity moves position towards the side to which you are leaning. Try it. What happens? As you lean across, your weight becomes increasingly transferred to the foot on whichever side you're leaning, and you'll feel your foot and lower leg fighting to keep you in a balanced position. As you lean further, your arm and leg on the side away from which you're leaning will start to move out away from you to help restore your balanced position – a classic counterbalance. Then you'll fall over. Unless of course you do what your body wants to do, which is to reposition your feet.

If you lean backwards from a standing position, you'll find that your hips and arms naturally move forwards, to act as a counterbalance to the centre of gravity, which has moved backwards from the stable platform provided by your feet, trying to keep your centre of gravity in a position in which you can remain upright.

Repeat this exercise leaning forwards and you'll find your feet and lower leg muscles tense to resist the change in centre of gravity, which has moved forwards and your arms move backwards to counterbalance. Hold a position where you are just

balanced, then slowly move your arms forwards – it doesn't take much arm movement to put you off balance again.

As a climber you're trying to defeat gravity! Gravity has the effect of pulling you back to the ground. It does so in an even-handed way, but you feel that pull through your centre of gravity.

In a climbing context, when you are in a balanced position, less force is required for you to maintain that position. A balanced position is one in which your body can more easily resist the force being applied to it by gravity through the centre of gravity. In climbing, it resists this force through the use of foot and handholds. It is ideal if you can move from one balanced position to another balanced position, even though the actual movement between these positions is unbalanced.

REMEMBER: your centre of gravity changes in a three-dimensional way, responding to arm and leg position changes, leaning backwards and forwards and crouching or stretching.

In the section on advanced climbing techniques, you'll see several examples of techniques that allow you to counterbalance when your centre of gravity is in an unusual position.

As a beginner, you'll find yourself using a limited range of techniques to start with, but it won't take long before you will be trying out the advanced techniques described later in this book.

Remember, one of the keys to good climbing is to know when to apply these techniques – it all depends on the relative positions and types of holds, the angle of the wall and your own physical make-up. Try them out in a controlled manner on bouldering walls and top roped climbs and don't worry if the techniques don't work on some moves – you learn as much from failure as success!

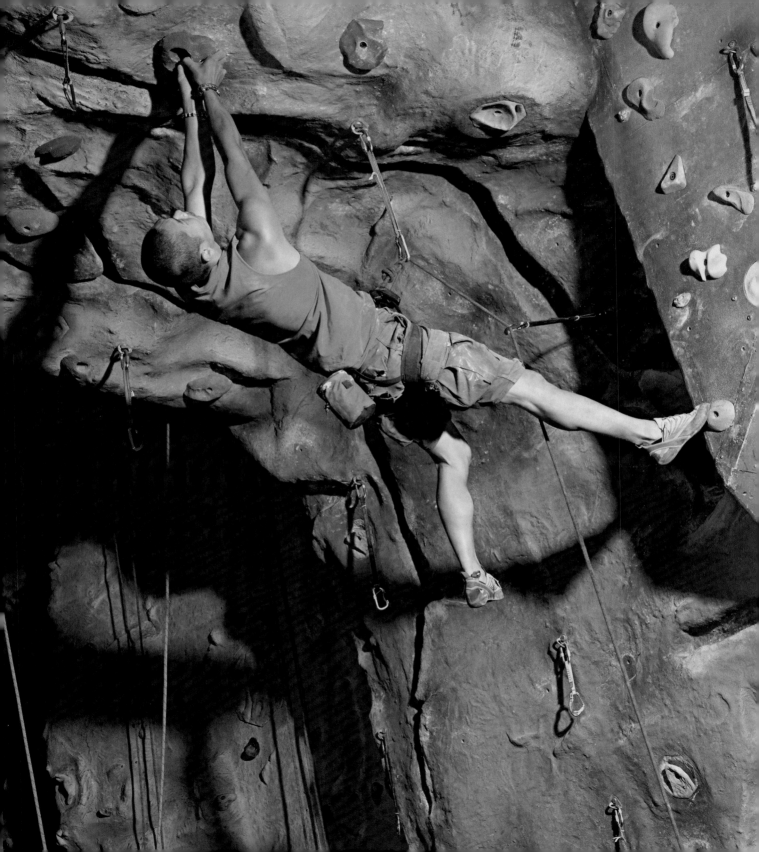

TOP
ROPE
CLIMBING

Indoor climbing is dangerous. You need to master a set of basic skills – known as top rope climbing – in order to climb safely. Learn and hone these skills with an instructor or an experienced climber.

Top roping is when the rope protects the climber from above, so in the event of a fall, it will hold the weight of the climber and prevent a fall taking place. The phrase 'top roping' also implies that the person belaying is at the top of the climb, which may occur in outdoor climbing. Where indoor climbing is concerned, with very few exceptions, the belayer will be at the bottom of the climb, with the rope running from the climber, through a top

▲ The fall arrest system in action. The climber has been held after a short fall while leading. You can see top ropes fixed to the left and many quickdraws for clipping while leading

anchor point – also called a lower off – and back down to the belay device, which is attached to the belayer's harness. Some people call this 'bottom roping' as the belayer is at the bottom of the climb.

THE FALL ARREST SYSTEM

The key to safety on the roped sectors of climbing walls is to understand the 'fall arrest system', and how to correctly use its different components. These include:

Harness A conventional sit harness allows the forces created in a fall or the climber's weight when lowering to be spread between waist, lower back and upper thighs. Full-body harnesses are available

▲ A section of wall set up for top roping at Reading Climbing Wall

and might be considered for climbers with back problems and certainly for younger children.

Rope A key component, the rope connects to the climber's harness at one end and to the belay device and belayer at the other. In the event of a fall, the rope stretches to absorb energy and reduces the shock-loading onto the climber and all other parts of the system including the belayer. The knot you use to tie in to your harness also plays a small part in shock absorption as it tightens when under load.

Belay device Allows the belayer to hold a fall or lower a climber in a controlled manner.

Belayer The belayer becomes part of the fall arrest system, as their control of the rope and position/movement in the event of a fall contributes towards reduced impact.

Top anchor The top anchor point, through which the rope runs when you are top roping with the belayer at the foot of the climb, forms part of the system. The friction of the rope through the top anchor reduces the forces to the belayer in a fall/lower.

Quickdraws On a climb in a straight line, the friction created by the rope running through each quickdraw is minimal, but frequently you'll see the lowest quickdraw being brought into play in the fall arrest system through the belayer choosing to position themselves at an angle to it, thus creating some friction.

It is important that each part of this system is used correctly to be fully effective. For normal top rope climbing the quickdraws are not involved.

GEARING UP

Most people 'gear up' in the changing area prior to a climb – this involves putting your harness and rock shoes on.

Harness

Your harness is a critical part of the fall arrest system and it should put you in a sitting position following a fall.

Putting your harness on becomes second nature very quickly, but you should always do the following:

- Check that you are following the manufacturer's instructions.
- Perform a quick check of your harness before use to ensure there is no damage. I had an almost brand

◄ A belayer using extra friction from the bottom quickdraw – a technique for experienced belayers only

▲ A modern, lightweight-climbing harness connected to a belay plate

new harness damaged by a mouse – the waistbelt was eaten halfway through, rendering it unusable, but it was only obvious on close inspection!

- If you're a beginner, get someone else to check your harness is fastened correctly before use.
- Ensure the tension of the waistbelt and leg loops is correct – as a guide you should be able to slip your thumbs down the waistbelt, but not your hands. A thumb down the side of the leg loop is fine. If it's too tight or too slack, it could alter the way the harness positions you in the event of a fall.
- Check that the leg loops are held in the correct position at the rear. The supporting straps should hold the leg loops quite high. If they are allowed to sit low on your thigh because the supporting straps are slack, you can end up tipping backwards in the event of a fall.
- Make sure the waistbelt is positioned at waist rather than hip level.
- Recheck the tension of both leg loops and harness before every climb and make sure any spare waistbelt is tucked in and not allowed to dangle.
- When using a waist buckle that you thread yourself, a good visual test is that if you can see the whole buckle it makes an 'O' shape – 'O' for 'open'. If it has been doubled back, it will show a 'C' shape – 'C' for 'closed'.
- Check your harness regularly for wear and fraying – the two points most at risk are the belay loop and the lower tie-in point (i.e. leg loop part).

Although it is extremely unusual for a harness to fail, there have been a small number of incidents in which a harness has failed due to the waistbelt not being fastened correctly – normally when the required final back threading of a buckle had not been completed. One such tragic case occurred in the States when well-known climber Todd Skinner died after his belay loop broke during an abseil. It was demonstrated that it was an old harness and its belay loop had excessive wear.

Constant vigilance is required on all harnesses to ensure they are fitted and fastened correctly in the first place and that they remain that way.

CHOOSING A ROUTE

You'll need to select a route to climb first – one which has a fixed top rope. At the foot of the wall, you'll find a small sign with details of the route colours matched with grades. For example, red holds might be designated a 5, Blue could be a 6b and using all the holds (Rainbow) might be 4+. You need to choose a route appropriate to your experience and standard. Start on easier climbs and see how you get on.

BEFORE YOU CLIMB

The rope

For top roping, the rope is already fixed, and will be checked regularly by the climbing wall staff. These ropes will often feel stiff and cumbersome compared to lead climbing ropes, but the principles of tying on and handling them remain the same. Before you tie on to your harness to climb, be sure to have a look at the route and decide which side of the lower off the climb is mostly on – you'll then tie into the end of the rope that hangs down that side.

Tying into your harness

The majority of climbers tie the rope to their harnesses using a figure-of-eight knot, but some climbers use a bowline. The reason for this is that a bowline is easier to untie than a figure-of-eight after being loaded, for example during a fall.

However, bowline knots have been known to fail when tied incorrectly – one recent indoor climbing wall fatality was sadly due to such a failure. In November 2012, John Long, one of America's best-known climbers, was seriously injured on an indoor wall in Los Angeles, when his bowline came untied and he fell to the floor. He suffered a compound fracture to his lower left leg/ankle.

Long attributes the accident to his own error; he forgot to finish his knot. 'I screwed up big,' he said. 'Double compound right at the ankle, and a big wound where the bone shot through. Long road back, but I'll make it.'

The figure-of-eight is reliable and, more importantly, it's easy to check that it's tied correctly. I would recommend this knot for tying into your harness.

It's a great idea to get your climbing partner to check your harness and knot for you, before you start climbing. I have witnessed several instances where climbers have set off on indoor routes with incomplete knots, simply due to the fact that they have been distracted when tying them. Doing this final check highlights issues before any damage can be done. Don't be left belaying a rope with no climber on the end! Buddy up and check.

Now you and your partner have put on your harnesses and the climber has tied on with a figure-of-eight knot. Next, we need to prepare to belay.

1 Start by tying a single eight knot into the rope about a metre from the end. If it looks like an eight it's correct. Thread the rope correctly through your harness attachment point and pull it until the single eight knot is close to your harness.

2 Thread the end of the rope back into the knot, starting by pushing it to the side of the point at which the rope first leaves the knot. Then, following this rope all the way back round the eight shape, finish with a short length of rope running parallel to the main climbing rope.

3 Check that the knot looks like a double eight and that there are no single ropes anywhere in the knot – they should all be double. The presence of a single rope means incorrect tying of the knot.

4 Finally, use the slack rope left over to tie a stopper knot, which finishes jammed up tight against the main eight knot. In the event of the knot tightening when in use due to a fall for example, you can usually slacken it by 'breaking' it open. This involves slackening the knot at the point furthest away from your harness by bending the knot apart.

AN INTRODUCTION TO BELAYING

Safe belaying is one of the most fundamental skills for a climber to possess, whether you're climbing indoors or outdoors, top roping or leading.

'Belaying' is the term given to the operation of a chosen safety system to allow the climber to be held in the event of a fall – whether leading or top roping. There are many different devices that allow you to do this and, especially when you climb outside, there are several different methods of using this equipment.

The key thing about belaying is that whatever device and system you use, you need to be able to hold your climbing partner's fall and, due to the key nature of this skill, failure to carry it out correctly can result in tragedy.

Connecting the belay plate

When I started climbing, I was introduced to 'waist belaying', where the rope wraps around your waist and also around the wrist of the arm that holds the rope leading to the coils, rather than the climber.

▲ Using a belay device is straightforward, but requires concentration

▲ Make sure both the rope and retaining strop are attached to the locking belay carabiner

This was standard practice and I enthusiastically joined in with training sessions during which we would hold the weight of a climber while the rope attempted to cut us in half. In the naivety of youth, I assumed that this would stand me in good stead when the real thing happened.

Some time later at Caley Crags in West Yorkshire, I had to hold my first real fall, while belaying at the top of a route – and it wasn't a pleasant experience! Holding, then lowering, my partner to the ground took all my effort and it was excruciatingly painful. The rope tied around my waist to which I had belayed back to a large boulder attempted to slice me from front to back, while the belaying rope, which anchored me to a large boulder, felt like a cheese wire, cutting me from back to front. There just had to be a better way!

Shortly after this experience, the first belay plate was made and, like most great designs, it was very simple – a flat, circular metal plate with two oval slots for use with single or double ropes – very similar to a modern belay device. It was called a Sticht Plate. It only took a couple of trial sessions to realise that this innovation was hugely significant and, combined with a harness, would make a massive contribution to increasing safety levels in climbing.

Although indoor belaying should be relatively straightforward and safe, there have been a number of belaying related accidents and many 'near misses'. The method of use for most static belay devices – the belay plates – is fundamentally the same (see below). You should read the instructions that come with the belay plate carefully and, if you are not confident about how to use it, get some help.

Other belay devices such as the Petzl Grigri and Click-Up are designed so that they will lock when loaded suddenly and their use is also covered below.

⌃ Auto-locking belay devices

How to belay for top roping

You're at the foot of the climb and the climber has tied onto the rope correctly. You, as belayer, take the rope where it comes down to the ground from the lower off and thread it correctly into your belay plate or other belay device, which is fastened to your harness via a lockable carabiner.

⌃ A correctly threaded belay plate

Belaying checklist

- Check both harnesses are fastened correctly.
- Check that the climber's knot is tied correctly.
- Check you have threaded the belay device correctly.
- Check the carabiner linking belay device to harness is locked.
- Check that you have the correct rope in the belay device!

STANCE

As belayer you need to be aware that in the event of a fall, even a very short one when top roping, the loading placed upon you can be considerable. You therefore have to stand in a stable position, close to the foot of the wall and just to the side of the line of the climber. You should adopt a braced position, with your feet slightly apart and with one foot in front of the other. The front foot should be the opposite one to whichever hand is operating the braking rope on the belay plate. You should feel that if someone tried to push you over, you could resist their force.

It's normal to stand slightly sideways so that the braking arm is away from the wall, so it has plenty of freedom of movement.

The climber should always check that you, the belayer, are ready before they start to climb. Most climbers say '*Climbing*!' as they set off and get an '*OK*' back from the belayer. A good position can be clearly seen in the photo.

⌄ A good belaying position close to the wall and just to the side of the climb

⌃ Keeping a close watch on the leader while paying rope out

The climb starts

Belayer Your job when top roping is to make sure the rope above the climber is neither slack nor tight. If it's too tight (unless the climber is struggling), it will upset the balance of the climber, while too slack means that in the event of a fall, the climber falls further than they should, thus risking potential injury, while the belayer is subjected to a much bigger force than should be the case. This in turn could lead to problems holding the climber. It also places more stress on your equipment and generally doesn't look good!

It's important to keep the rope snug on the climber for the first few metres of the climb, as a fall from a low height can result in the climber hitting the floor due to rope stretch.

Note As your partner climbs, slack rope will be generated in the system, which you have to take in through the belay plate at a speed appropriate to the climber's ascent. Sometimes you may have to feed some slack out if the climber wants to descend a little.

How to take in using a belay plate

Start with the rope locked, your top hand a short way above belay plate, your bottom hand (the 'braking' hand) locked down beneath the plate, holding the rope firmly. Don't put your top hand too high on the rope – keep each taking in movement quite short and this will make the process more manageable.

Once you have either reached the limit of your movement or taken in as much slack rope as is available, you have to rearrange your hands. To do this, first bring the braking hand straight back down to your thigh (if your right hand is the braking hand it will come back to your right thigh).
Note The movement of the braking hand from its locked position, pushed upwards to take in slack rope and down again to its original position is completed as one swift movement. Do not leave your braking hand positioned above the belay plate.

As the climber moves up, start taking in slack rope by pushing upwards with your braking hand. Immediately after you start to push upwards, help the rope by pulling down with your top hand. **Note** If you pull down with your top hand before you push up with your braking hand, you'll end up with a loop of rope which makes taking in more difficult.

Make the taking-in movement quick and strong and complete it even if the amount of rope to be taken in is small.

You'll notice that your top hand is now close to the belay plate and needs to be repositioned. To do this safely, bring your top hand down to grip the rope immediately beneath the belay plate, then slide your braking hand up the rope to meet it.

Grip the rope with your braking hand and move your top hand back above the belay plate to resume your original position as in the first photo of the sequence.

This method ensures that at no time is the braking rope beneath the belay plate left without at least one hand gripping it. You must never let go of the braking rope and you must never leave the braking rope above the belay plate.

AUTO-LOCKING DEVICES

There are several very popular auto-locking belaying devices on the market that are designed for single rope sport climbing, the best-known of which is the Grigri. These tend to be used mostly by experienced climbers who have a full understanding of the dynamics of belaying. Although they should lock under a sudden load, they are not hands-free devices!

Each device has its own set of instructions, and you must read and understand them fully before using the device. It's also worth checking manufacturers' websites and the main climbing forums for updates.

To use a Grigri for top roping, your hands operate in a similar way as they would with a normal belay plate – one hand either side of the device, and the braking hand never lets go. Your top hand pushes rope out to provide slack to a leader

▲ Slack rope above climber

and your bottom hand helps by feeding rope into the device. You don't have to perform the hand change as described for the belay plate – your hands simply slide along the rope.

There is a common misconception that these devices offer a failsafe, no hands auto-lock facility, so that a falling climber will always be held regardless of the situation. As for the belay plate – never let go of the braking rope.

Climber If you're climbing quickly and you see slack rope above you because the belayer can't take in quickly enough, pause and let the belayer catch up.

Belayer Concentrate! It's easy to get distracted, chatting to mates or watching someone else climb. There's no doubt that distraction has led to a number of accidents, so stay focused and watch the climber all the time!

For using belay devices of any sort, make sure you only use the information provided by the manufacturer. I came across this very misleading piece of advice on a climbing website: 'In order to

▾ Don't get distracted when you're belaying

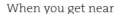
◄ A good lowering position: sit back into the harness, feet apart and look down at where you're going

➤ Make sure your hands are both on the braking rope before you start lowering with a belay plate

sit back onto the rope. Once your lower has started, lean back, look over your shoulder to see where you're going and walk down.

When you get near the ground, make sure you step down at the right moment in order to end up in a standing position.

Belayer When the climber is at the top of the route or as far up as they can go, you'll need to lower them back down. To do this, first make sure that the rope is quite tight between you and the climber before lowering commences. Then, move your top hand down to join your bottom hand on the rope below the belay plate, so that both hands are in control of the descent.

Tell the climber to lean back. When you have the climber's weight on the rope, start to slowly let the rope out, increasing the speed slightly once the climber is fully into the lowering position and is established on the descent. Keep both hands on the braking rope and alter the speed by adjusting the amount of grip your hands exert on the rope, coupled with the angle at which the rope is held. (The greater the angle you hold the rope back at, the slower the descent).

Note As the climber descends, be prepared for the force you feel to be greater as they get lower.

Make the lower as smooth as possible, keep watching the climber and when they get close to the ground, keep a constant speed to help them judge when to step to the ground. Be prepared to

stop a climber's fall, you will need to quickly give slack to the climber.' *This is not the case!*

Belayer and climber Make sure you communicate with each other. Enjoy the climb!

Lowering a climber

Climber Stop just below the lower-off point – don't climb past it. You should ensure that you are happy that your belayer is ready to lower you before you

▲ Lowering with a Grigri　　　➤ Using a ground anchor

Belaying a heavier climber

If your climbing partner is only slightly heavier than you, then you should be able to control their descent satisfactorily, as the friction through the top anchor reduces the force. If there is a substantial difference between the weight of the (heavy) climber and the (light) belayer, then you need to take action to prevent the belayer from being subjected to forces that could lead to discomfort or even loss of control.

The main method of doing this is to clip the belay loop of the belayer's harness into a suitable floor anchor – effectively making the belaying climber heavier. At many climbing walls, weights are provided (typically this could be a small barrel of sand), which you can clip into the belay loop of your harness and which helps to prevent you being lifted off the ground by the weight of a heavier climber. There is a limit to the weight difference between belayer and climber beyond which it becomes unsafe.

The other thing to consider regarding belaying a heavier climber is that it is important to ensure

lock the rope if they misjudge this. Some beginners will keep leaning back even when nearly on the ground, and end up in a heap on the floor – can be quite amusing, but equally could hurt! They may also step down too soon and have a close encounter between their nose and the wall – the touch down has to be judged well by both climber and belayer.

BELAYER: LOWERING WITH A GRIGRI

Make sure the climber is ready to be lowered as already described, then, keeping the braking hand on the rope, use your other hand to pull the lever to release the locking cam. Find a balanced position using the lever and the braking hand to provide a controlled descent. Never release the braking rope and keep hold of the lever, or the lowering climber will simply fall.

Belayer Both the climber and the equipment will thank you for a smooth descent!

that the belay plate/rope diameter is appropriate. Clearly a smaller person could have increased difficulty in holding a heavier climber generally, but this can be made even more difficult if a thin rope is used with a slick belay plate, when the actual physical difficulty of keeping hold of the rope in the event of a fall is increased.

Dealing with top rope falls

Belayer If a fall happens, you will need to immediately lock the braking rope to stop it and take the climber's weight. This will be done with the braking hand on the braking rope below the belay plate in the locked position and with the other hand holding the rope above the belay plate. Once you have the fall under control, bring the top hand down onto the braking rope. Keep tight hold of the braking rope with both hands until the climber has told you whether they want to be lowered down or continue climbing, then either lower them down or revert to belaying if they intend to continue climbing. With a Grigri, the device should lock in the event of a fall, but retain hold of the braking rope.

If you have never held a fall, you may want to try doing so in a limited, controlled situation. Make sure you have someone to take hold of the controlling rope from the belay plate behind you – a buddy system, so that they can lock it should you fail to do so.

Ask your climber to stop a short way up the climb and then to slump his/her weight onto the rope when you're ready for him/her to do so. This will introduce you to the feel of a climber's weight. If this is OK you might want to try a short, controlled slip onto the rope on a part of the wall where this will not cause injury – a gently overhanging portion of wall is ideal. This might also be a useful controlled test to perform when using a new belay device/rope combination, to ensure you're prepared for a real fall.

Climber If you fall, the belayer will hold you. Decide whether you want to be lowered or if you want to continue. Make sure the belayer understands your intention.

Top roping overhanging walls

If you're top roping overhanging walls, the climbing rope must be clipped into each of the quickdraws above the climber. This is so that in the event of a fall, you only fall a short distance away from the wall. If only the lower-off point was clipped (fine for slabs and vertical walls) and you fell off near the foot of the climb, you would swing a long way outwards and possibly collide with other wall users.

As you climb, unclip each quickdraw as you come to it. If the rope is a fixed one, when you are being lowered, stop by each quickdraw and reclip the rope to each one.

⌄ Using a buddy to belay with – ideal if you're a backing up a beginner or for testing a short fall onto the rope

6

LEAD
CLIMBING
INDOORS

BELAYING
A LEAD CLIMBER

Lead climbing indoors is relatively simple compared to normal outdoor climbing because you do not have to place your own protection. Instead, bolts are placed at close intervals, to which you either clip your own quickdraw and rope or clip your rope into fixed quickdraws, depending on the system in place.

The bolts are placed and clipped frequently, reducing the chance of a significant fall. Although it's all really quite straightforward, there are still a number of things that can go wrong so, as always, concentration is essential.

I'm assuming by this stage that you've already mastered the skills involved in top roping as discussed in previous chapters.

From my experience of watching people belay at indoor walls, the standard of belaying is generally very variable. Often, too much slack is left in the rope, increasing the distance that the climber could fall, and the belayer's concentration is often focused on matters other than the leader. Climbing walls report many near-miss accidents and a good proportion of these are as a result of poor belaying skills and a simple lack of attention.

As the lead climber ascends, they will clip into the fixed protection points as they go. Rather like the belayer's job in top roping, your job here is also to make sure that first, you're in the correct position and second, the rope between you and the climber is neither slack nor tight. This is more difficult to achieve: the rope may need to be paid out very quickly one moment and taken in the next, for

⌄ A fall can be sudden and the belayer must be alert and ready

◄ There's too much slack in the system here – a slip at this point would end up with a ground fall

▲ Leader and belayer work as a team to ensure successful clipping

example, when the leader clips above them.

If the rope is too slack and the leader falls, they could face a considerably longer fall then they should have, which places more stress on the whole fall arrest system. This can, in turn, place an uncomfortable, or even dangerously, large force on the belayer. If the fall were to occur low down on the climb, the climber could even hit the ground. Having too much slack in the system is not to be confused with a 'dynamic belay' (see page 84).

Alternatively, if the rope is too tight, the lead climber can't move freely enough and will find it difficult to take rope to clip the protection. This means more hanging around for the leader with a consequent loss of strength and loss of confidence in the belayer.

If you watch an experienced team climbing, you'll notice how smooth, almost effortless the protection clipping is. The belayer and leader work as a team to make sure everything is fast and smooth. In turn, this increases the chance of a successful and safe ascent as little strength is lost in waiting for the belayer to give slack rope. Confidence levels are, therefore, high because the leader trusts the second.

Some key points for the belayer:

- *Total concentration at all times.*
- You must constantly watch the climber's movements and anticipate the payout or take-in of rope, making slight adjustments all the time to compensate accordingly.
- You should stand in a braced position at the foot of the wall and just to the side of the line of the climber – ready to hold a fall.

CLIPPING

The next point relates to when the climber clips into a quckdraw. As belayer you have to be ready to provide the right amount of slack rope at just the right time. So, keep watching the climber and his/her position in relation to the next clip. If the c.limber starts to pull rope for the clip when he/she is below it, you know you'll need to provide quite a bit of rope – and fast. If the climber is next to the clip, you may only need to provide a small amount of slack. Knowledge of the route might help in terms of anticipating this. You'll also learn to anticipate where a climber will clip from, based on the layout and size of the holds and the climber's movements.

Here are a couple of tips to help make sure the lead climber never feels the rope tighten between the two of you, creating that feeling of being held back. First, keep a small amount of slack – maybe 15–30cm – between your top hand and the climber. This gives you a little play, which allows for the initial pull up of rope by the climber and also gives you a little time to react and pay out some more slack.

Down below the belay device on the braking rope, keep a small amount of slack – maybe 15cm – between your hand and the belay device. As soon as you see the climber moving up he/she will use the slack above your top hand, which will then feel the climber starting to move, so move your top hand upwards, feeding rope out. This takes up any slack you have between the belay device and your locking hand. This, in turn, gives an immediate production of slack rope to the leader, who feels no rope tightness or drag. It also gives you a second or so to rearrange your hands and pay out more slack as required.

Using this method, if a fall were to occur, the bottom hand immediately goes into a braking position, so the slack there is instantly removed from the system, and the only additional slack added to the fall is the few centimetres of rope above the belay device.

˅ Keeping a small amount of slack in the rope, and altering your position in relation to the bottom of the wall, enables you to feed rope or take in more quickly, but care should be taken not to give too much slack

Second, more experienced belayers also frequently move further from the bottom of the wall as the climber gains height. They then move backwards or forwards a little to provide some slack or to take in. Great care should be exercised in doing this to ensure a leader fall does not cause the belayer to stumble or fall.

If you're belaying using a Grigri, it can be difficult to give slack rope to the leader quickly enough for 'panic clips'. You can give rope more quickly by keeping hold of the braking rope and using your thumb to push down over the top of the device to release the cam. This is not easy and requires practice.

Note

Do not remove your braking hand from the rope to release the cam for a quicker feed through on a Grigri! Look on www.petzl.com for more details.

You'll see some belayers leaving a lot of slack rope above the belay device and top hand, all of which will add to the distance a climber could fall and the eventual loading on the system. This is not recommended. This practice does not create a dynamic belay effect, it simply increases the forces felt by the belayer and climber and the climber ends up falling further. Some people say they are doing this deliberately to lengthen the climber's fall and avoid the problem of slamming back into the wall, which can be an issue with a sudden, short fall. In fact, this can be done by adding a dynamic element to the belay system (see overleaf) rather than just introducing a random amount of slack.

It's important to understand that when indoor climbing, there is little friction created in the system to help reduce the forces involved in the event of a fall. By contrast, in outdoor climbing, it's often the case that the rope runs around and over the rock surface and through protection points that are less

▲ A belayer pulled off the ground during a leader fall

regularly positioned than on an indoor wall. This creates extra friction, which often reduces the forces felt by the belayer in a leader fall. The point is that the forces felt by the belayer in a leader fall on an indoor wall will often be higher than those experienced in a fall when outdoor climbing. So, in spite of the relatively benign indoor climbing environment and the relative feeling of safety engendered, falls may be harder to hold than you expect and your concentration levels need to be spot on.

No extra slack

As belayer, you need to be aware that low down on the climb, up to third bolt level, in particular, there is a real need to ensure that there is no extra slack in the system due to the possibility of it allowing the climber to hit the ground in the event of a fall.

DYNAMIC BELAYING

In a leader fall situation, we are concerned about the overall force created, the ability of the equipment we use to reduce this force and the effects that all this has on climber, belayer and equipment.

In a normal fall situation on an indoor wall, the belayer will lock-off the braking rope on the belay plate and the force created in the fall will be partially dissipated by the stretch of the rope, the contraction of the knot and any slippage of the rope, through the belay plate, along with any movement of the belayer either upwards or towards the foot of the wall. While it's generally good to hold a fall quickly, it can lead to the lead climber swinging suddenly back into the wall and possibly sustaining injury, as a result.

Dynamic belaying involves adding another dimension to this. The belayer deliberately either allows a small amount of slippage of the rope through the belay plate in a controlled manner or moves towards the wall/upwards towards the climber to reduce the impact.

The effect of this is that the climber falls slightly further, the impact force is reduced and the climber is less likely to swing back into the wall.

In practice, this is hard to achieve via the belay plate, as the natural reaction of the belayer in the event of a fall is to immediately lock the rope off.

It is easier for an experienced belayer to achieve a dynamic belay by moving towards the wall at the moment of the fall or aiding the reduction in shock loading by deliberately jumping upwards slightly from a position beneath the climber.

Dynamic belaying can only be carried out when the climber is higher than about fourth or fifth bolt level to make sure that they don't fall too far and hit the ground.

In an indoor wall situation, you should try to receive instruction in the use of dynamic belaying. Quite simply, when performed incorrectly, it can be dangerous.

▲ Dynamic belaying in action

Experienced climbers use a range of tactics to make the belay more dynamic, but they may also have problems associated with them. A good example would be that some climbers move well away from the foot of the wall when the climber is above the 3rd or 4th bolt. In the event of a fall, they are pulled back towards the wall by the force created and this, in theory, reduces the shock loading and, therefore, makes the belay more dynamic. However, accidents have occurred during which a belayer standing away from the foot of the wall has been pulled more violently than expected towards the wall – particularly if distraction has been involved – thus resulting in a loss of control and a potentially serious fall for the leader. This technique is a good one for effecting dynamic belays, but should only be used with care by experienced belayers.

If you belay with a Grigri, you can't allow controlled slippage through the device in the event of a fall – you have to use the alternative techniques mentioned above to create a dynamic belay.

Lowering the leader following a fall or after reaching the top is the same as for top roping once the leader has clipped into the lower-off point.

You'll need to take care when lowering the climber that other people are not standing in the landing zone.

LEAD CLIMBING INDOORS: THE LEADER

Style

You'll hear people referring to several different styles of lead climbing – here are the main ones.
On-sight This means climbing the route without resting or falling and with no prior knowledge of the climb, other than what you can see from standing on the ground.
Flash To climb a route without practising the moves, but with some prior knowledge (prior knowledge is often known as 'Beta').
Redpoint If you redpoint a route, you climb it without falling, but after some degree of inspection and rehearsing the moves. An on-sight ascent is placed highest in the order of desirability for a leader, but most people redpoint routes as a regular part of their climbing. For sought-after outdoor climbs, the on-sight ascent can be very precious.

Preparation

In order to prepare properly, first take a good look at the route and glean whatever information you can about the hold layout, resting places, and so on. Then, if the quickdraws are not in place, count the number of bolts on the route so you know how many quickdraws to take. Check the route length in relation to your rope. It's unlikely to be too short,

but a 50m rope on a 25m wall, after tying on? With rope stretch you should be fine but if in doubt just tie a knot in the end of the rope to stop the end slipping through the belay plate. This is often done in outdoor sport climbing on long routes. Better still though, use a longer rope!

Make sure your quickdraws are arranged conveniently on your harness, taking into account what you can see of the climb and to which side of your body you are likely to clip. If the route is mostly to the left of the bolts line, you will carry most of your quickdraws on your right.

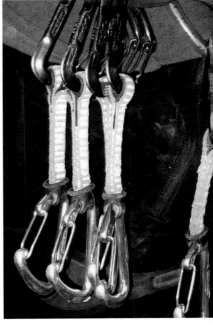

▲ Carabiners arranged correctly on quickdraws

Make sure your quickdraw carabiners are clipped correctly for easy clipping. The best and most usual format is the carabiner at the top of the quickdraw being clipped onto your gear loop with the gate facing your body and the opening part of the gate at the top. The other carabiner (into which the rope will be clipped) is positioned so that the gate opens in the opposite direction to the top carabiner and the opening part of the gate is at the bottom. This means that after you clip the quickdraw into the bolt, the movement to clip the rope into the quickdraw is exactly the same.

The rope

The last thing you want when you lead a route is to find your rope tangled and twisted, with the belayer shouting up for you to hang on a minute while he/she tries to untangle it. Make sure it's uncoiled correctly and ready to use. Using a rope bag is the easiest way to ensure that this happens when you're climbing indoors (see page 26).

Inspect your rope Most people don't bother, but it is a good idea always to check your rope for damage, knots and twists before you start climbing. Running through the rope from one end to the other, dropping the rope as you go through it and feeling it as you pull it through your hand to check for damage is good practice, as is undertaking a visual check.

Clipping – when to clip

One of the key skills in lead climbing is knowing when to clip the next bolt. As you climb, you need to be constantly aware of the consequences of a fall. Try to watch other people climbing (and falling) and see what happens. As a general rule, the fall will always be further than you imagined it would be

and you'll see some climbers fall quite a long way when they are very close to a bolt.

The first three bolts, in particular, need to be clipped carefully. Think: 'What if I fall?' when you're doing this. It may seem logical that you should try to clip the next bolt when you are still below it to give you maximum protection as you move up to it and then past it. *But* have a think about this for a moment and consider the following scenario.

You're two bolts up and looking to clip the third, which is still above you. You decide to pull some rope through and clip it while you are still beneath it, so you pull rope through, reach high and just as you're clipping it, a foot slips and you fall. Because you've pulled up enough rope to clip the next bolt above you, there could easily be 2m of slack rope, which, in turn, could result in a fall of several metres once you've added on rope stretch and slippage. If you're below the third bolt you can probably see where this is going: to the ground.

◄ Reaching up to clip the third bolt

▲ A fall while clipping would result in a ground fall

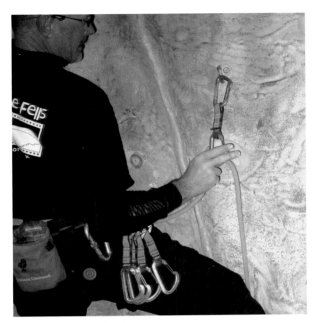

▲ Clipping at waist level

clips in. You then have to reach down and pull the rope up to clip into the other, lower carabiner. If your carabiners are aligned correctly, you'll use the same movement to both clip your quickdraw to the bolt and to clip your rope to the quickdraw.

In almost all situations, the carabiner to which you clip your rope will be hanging so that it is flat against the wall. It therefore has a front and a back. To clip your rope correctly you need to ensure it is clipped from the back, to the front. This ensures that there is virtually no chance of any fall resulting in the rope coming undone from the carabiner.

▲ The quickdraw here has been correctly clipped: the rope runs from the back of the carabiner to the front

The alternative would have been to make another move or two and clip when the bolt is at waist level next to your harness. Even though you've climbed higher, there would be less rope between you and the next bolt down if you fell while clipping.

When to clip, then, depends on several factors, the most important being how far up the climb you are and the physical difficulty associated with stopping to clip – and this will depend on the size and layout of the holds at that point of the climb. Making an extra move up could make the clip much easier, and may be in fact safer than trying to clip from below, in the middle of a difficult move.

How to clip

If there are no quickdraws in place, you'll need to clip your own to the bolts before clipping your rope in. This is relatively easy, and involves taking the quickdraw off your harness, then pushing the gate of the carabiner against the bolt so it opens and

Watch how experienced climbers clip into quickdraws and try to copy their techniques. You'll see several different methods depending on which hand is doing the clipping and to which side the quickdraw gate opening hangs.

The most common method is to clip with the right hand to a carabiner that is opening on its right side or with the left hand to a carabiner opening on its left.

The reverse clip is when you clip with the opposite hand to that described above. It all depends on how the holds at that point on the climb allow you to move.

▾ Some climbers use their thumb to push the rope past the gate of the carabiner

> A correct clip

Most people place their thumb on the back of the carabiner so that they have something to push against when clipping the rope in. It's also common to stabilise the base of the carabiner with the middle finger, while the other fingers clip the rope in.

Becoming fast and proficient at clipping the rope into the quickdraws and, indeed, clipping the quickdraws to the bolts if you need to is essential to be able to lead at a higher standard. Quick clipping reduces energy expenditure and leaves you feeling more confident and strong. It also keeps the 'flow' of the climb going.

Practise to become a master slick-clipper.

Problems with clipping

BACKCLIPPING

Quickdraws should be clipped so the rope runs from the belayer, between the wall and the clipping carabiner and out away from the wall to the climber's harness. If you clip your rope the opposite way: from the front to back, you stand a very small chance of the rope disconnecting itself from the carabiner in the event of a fall.

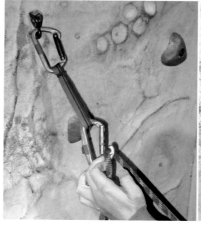

▲ You should avoid clipping the rope from front to back (the rope to the climber's harness is on the right)

▲ It is possible for the rope to run across the gate of the carabiner and disconnect

▲ It is possible to clip incorrectly by pulling the rope up from below the previous quickdraw, resulting in a Z-clip. If you do this, you have to leave the top quickdraw in place and reclip the next one down.

Z-CLIP

Another common beginners' error is to 'z-clip'. This involves clipping the wrong part of the rope into the quickdraw by reaching down and taking slack rope from beneath the previous bolt, rather than from above it. This creates a 'Z' shape in the rope and means that the rope runs through the upper clip, back to the next clip down and then to your harness.

LOWERING

Once the leader reaches the top, they first clip into the lower off. Many walls have two lower-off carabiners side by side. The one with an open gate, you clip first. The second has a locking gate. You can clip your rope into this second carabiner and lock its gate knowing you are already clipped into the first.

It is normal for the leader to be lowered to the ground as described in chapter 5. If no more of your party are climbing the route, the last person down should remove any quickdraws you placed and 'clean' the route. You wouldn't need to do this, however, if the quickdraws are pre-placed. If another member of your party is climbing the route, it's usual to leave the quickdraws in place and pull the rope down, although some people prefer to redo the whole thing. It's a matter of personal choice.

If you fall off

You're going to take a leader fall sooner or later. If it happens, you can get lowered back to the ground, but you may want to get back onto the wall and continue the climb. On easier angled routes this is not a problem; however, on overhanging walls you may not be able to reach the wall following a fall.

You can try and swing back into the wall by generating a swinging momentum until you reach a hold – or, if it's really steep, you can pull on the rope that runs back down from the top quickdraw to the belayer, if you can reach it. After each pull, the belayer has to take the slack rope in and can even help you by pulling down at the same time as you do, so you have to work in conjunction with him/her. It's hard work, but you should be able to pull enough to get back to the top quickdraw and start again.

Awareness of other users

It's really important to be very aware of what other people are doing at the wall, as they can be a danger to you, and vice versa. Classic examples include lower offs on overhanging sections where the climber being lowered ends up some distance from the foot of the wall. There is a responsibility on the part of the belayer to ensure the climber is not lowered onto someone else and other users also need to ensure that they have noted of the position

of other climbers being lowered. Three-dimensional awareness is essential – you're on the look-out for danger from above as well as to the sides, in front and to the rear.

If you're being lowered, be aware that there may be other climbers on nearby lines, possibly leading, who could be at risk from you – keep to a direct line beneath the lower off to avoid sideways swings and possible interference with other climbers.

On some busy climbing walls, climbers are packed perilously close together on line after line. Be aware of the position of other climbers in relation to yourself and make sure your actions don't impede or even cause injury to other climbers close by.

COMMUNICATION

Communication is critical in outdoor climbing and it is still very important when climbing indoors. Though there are many established systems of communication in rock climbing, you'll also find that regular climbing partners devise their own variations.

Communication for indoor climbing is simpler than for outdoor in terms of the range of terminology used, although it can be difficult to hear your climbing partner sometimes, especially on bigger, busier walls. Fortunately, most of the time, you have better visual contact than in outdoor climbing and that can be really useful. As with outdoor climbing, the important thing is that you and your climbing partner are tuned into the same climbing language and always understand what the other is saying.

At very least, it's usual for the climber and belayer to agree everything is ready before the climb commences, and for the climber to say 'climbing' when they set off. You also need a clear understanding of what's going on when the lead climber is high on the wall. Different people have different systems for communication, sometimes

using sign language. A grunt and a nod is also good enough for many wall users!

However you decide to communicate, you need to be certain that you understand exactly what your partner wants.

Common terms include:

'Tight' This usually means that the climber is going to fall off and wants the rope as tight as possible.

'Slack' This means the climber wants you to feed them slack rope. Often shouted when pulling rope up to clip.

'Take in' This means there is too much slack in the system and the belayer needs to take in and get rid of it.

> **Do nots**
>
> Don't shout 'Take in the slack'. Your partner may only hear the 'slack' part of it and do the opposite to what you intended!

'OK' This can mean pretty much anything you want, so make sure you understand exactly what your climbing partner is trying to tell you!

As mentioned above, you normally have excellent visual communication with your climbing partner on an indoor wall, so use this in conjunction with verbal communication to make sure you understand each other clearly.

CONCENTRATION

This has already been mentioned, but it is so important to remain completely focused. Typical scenarios that can break your concentration include chatting to friends at the bottom of climbs, watching someone else climb nearby, an incident, such as a fall taking place elsewhere on the wall or simply being caught up people-watching. Lack of concentration is frequently a contributory factor in accidents, so beware!

7

Advanced Climbing Techniques

It's fascinating to see how climbing techniques have evolved and been honed over the years to new levels. Equally, it's surprising to see how many of the modern 'advanced' techniques have actually been around for a long time, but perhaps without the terminology we use today.

Nothing new

I can remember watching the late Pete Livesey perform figure-of-four manoeuvres at Rothwell in the 1970s and I've never seen anyone repeat his gymnastic move to finish off the roof climb there, which involved a backwards somersault onto the ledge! Climbers have used 'Gastons' and 'flagged' with their legs for years, without recording the skills by name, so there are actually relatively few genuinely innovative recent technical developments – rather a more generalised honing, naming and tightening of techniques.

This chapter covers very specific techniques as well as including some more general advice on overcoming specific types of harder climbing problems, such as 'roof'. There are also some useful general principles to help you to climb harder routes with less energy expenditure and in better style.

Let's start by looking at a range of more specific advanced techniques, beginning with a technique named after a master climber.

GASTON

Named after the great French climber Gaston Rébuffat, who used this technique on cracks, a 'Gaston' is simply a sidepull used as if you were trying to open the doors of a lift by hand. Most people use it as a one-hand move, but sometimes, especially in crack climbing, both hands are used in a 'Double Gaston'. It's a common move when you're traversing and you could liken it to a standard layback/sidepull hold, but reversed. Once again the layout of the holds determines the usefulness of the move.

FROGGING

The frog position is very much as it sounds – the climber uses the body a bit like a frog would. As with all techniques, it has to be applied to the most appropriate situation and then carried out correctly for it to be successful. One of the key benefits of the frog position is that it enables you to get your hips close into the wall and therefore take more weight through your feet. Applied on overhanging walls,

⌄ Adam Lincoln performing a 'Gaston' move with his right arm

▲ Dave Birkett demonstrates the frog position from a single foothold

➤ Ellen Spencer demonstrates a semi-frog. This position enables you to get your hips really close into the wall and get more weight over your foot

it is possible to move from the frog position into a dynamic move by pushing upwards with your legs at the same time as pulling with your arms, but the leg push has to be upwards and not outwards. This demands very high levels of flexibility and good coordination. It may also be good for using one larger foothold.

SEMI-FROG

This position is more common and involves using only one leg in the squat position, while the other leg trails below. Used where there is a single foothold and often in conjunction with low handholds, it can help the climber achieve a balanced position with the hips pushed tightly against the wall. It's often used as a rest position or as a stable position from which to clip. It can also provide the basis for a dynamic move.

Frog positions do place considerable strain through the knee joint and care must be taken to ensure that you have the flexibility and strength to perform these moves safely.

HEEL HOOKING

The use of your heel for hooking holds is an old technique and your rock boot has a high section of rubber around the heel to help with grip. Often used in the past for helping rest on steep walls when the types of hold allowed, it's also frequently used now as the first stage in a rockover move (see page 62), when the heel hook is turned into a high foothold

▲ This sequence shows the use of a heel hook turned into a foothold. The second photo shows a heel/hand share

as the climber moves higher on the problem. Heel hooks are also great for helping to prevent body swing when traversing and can add significant stability to a move. They can also provide another means of pulling, as downwards force is applied through the heel. Heel hooking requires good core strength in order to obtain the initial heel position.

TOE HOOKING

You can hook with your toe as well as your heel. Whereas a 'heel hook' is normally applied over the top of a hold, a 'toe hook' is generally applied to the side of, or sometimes underneath, a hold. Tension is applied through the toes and lower leg to exert a force on the hold, while predominantly upper leg and hip muscles hold the limb in position. Once again, using toe hooks requires good core strength.

➤ Using a toe hook to retain balance and stop feet swinging under the overhang until the best hand positions have been located

▲ Sharing a handhold with a toe hook

▶ Dave Birkett using a toe hook to pull across

Toe hooking can also be used as a means of pulling the body across and even upwards, if you're flexible enough.

BICYCLING

It would be unusual to find holds that allowed the use of this technique on real rock, but some climbing wall holds are made for it. Whatever foot is on top of the hold applies the usual downward force, while the other foot is placed beneath the same hold and pulls in an upward direction, locking the body in position better. This technique allows you to take a little more weight off your arms and helps hold your hips into the wall when reaching up for the next handhold.

▶ A bicycling move in which one foot stands on the hold and the other pulls up underneath it

▲ This flagging move is aiming to create a centre of gravity beneath the climber's left hand, to make the next reach easier

FLAGGING

Used by climbers for generations, this counterbalance technique involves using the inactive leg to alter your weight distribution and centre of gravity. Applied correctly, it allows you to relieve the weight on your arms sufficiently to reach the next hold, simply by improving the balance of your position through adjusting your centre of gravity.

Types of flagging

Normal flag The most common technique. The leg that you are flagging is out to the same side – that is, if you have your right foot on a foothold and place your left foot out to the left it's a normal flag. The left foot can be smeared or is perhaps more commonly in the air at whatever position counterbalances best.

Reverse flag The leg that you are flagging is crossed behind the leg on the foothold. If you have your left foot on a foothold, you would cross your right leg behind your left leg.

Arm flag Occasionally you also flag with your inactive arm, once again aiming to apply a counterbalance to improve your positional stability.

Flagging can be used on rock of all angles, through to overhangs and extended roof climbs.

TWIST LOCKING AND BACKSTEPPING

The 'twist lock' combined with a 'backstep' remains one of the key methods of making moves on overhanging walls. The steeper the wall, the harder it is to take weight on your feet, and the more weight comes onto your arms, which are of course weaker. Using a twist lock and backstep pulls your body in towards the wall – especially through the hips – thus allowing you to take more weight through your feet.

▲ Dave Birkett demonstrates the use of flagging to complete a mantelshelf move

▲ Ian Williamson demonstrating a simple twist lock and backstep position, which make it easier to reach high for the next hold

➤ Twist locking is useful, even on very steep problems

The twist lock is typically used to make a reach up easier on overhanging moves. For example, your right hand is on a good hold and you'd like to reach up high with the left hand. While you could attempt this move straight on with your chest facing toward the wall, it's much less strenuous to turn your left hip into the wall before making the reach upward. Good positioning of the feet is essential for making this move work. As your left hip is turning to the wall, you'll need to use the outside edge of your left foot on a hold somewhere below or behind your body – this is the backstepping bit of the move. Usually you'll find a complementary right foothold to help maintain the twist lock body position. The feet then press in opposition to each other while the right arm pulls down and in toward your body, creating the twist lock. Finding the correct body position in relation to the holds on offer is the key to obtaining a secure twist lock. It's a very efficient technique and one of the staple moves of climbing steep walls.

This move is closely related to the 'drop knee' move described below, which is a more extreme version of the same basic principle. Also known as an 'Egyptian'.

DROP KNEE

A 'drop knee' is a more advanced stage of twist locking. For example, if you put your right foot out to the right and it is placed as a backstep, then your knee will be pointing in towards you rather than away from you. If your foot is higher than where your knee normally would be and you turn your knee in and down then this represents a classic drop knee.

This technique is very useful for holding your hips against the wall on steeper climbs and getting more weight onto your feet.

To try this, find a slightly overhanging wall and start on two straight pull-down holds that are about shoulder-width apart. Place your left foot on a foothold directly below the handholds at a comfortable distance. Take your right foot and place it between knee and hip height out to the right. Turn your right knee in and down and try to pull your right hip against the wall. This should make it easier for you to reach up and across with your right hand. Do the same thing out to the left. The knee position allows you to twist your hip close to the wall, helping take more weight and making a reach easier. You'll find foot rotation is a key element of the technique.

⌄ A demonstration of a perfect knee drop at Northampton Climbing Wall

➤ Nick Warton, demonstrating an outside-edge move. Note how the outside of the right foot is used in conjunction with a sidepull and a left-foot flag to give an easy reach up

OUTSIDE EDGE MOVE

Turning side on to the wall and using the outside edge of your foot can enable you to make long reaches, especially from sidepulls and undercuts. This move also puts your hip close into the rock, but you need to be careful that you don't 'barndoor' – swing outwards from your handhold. The opposite foot frequently flags to counterbalance.

KNEE BAR

This is a really useful method of getting a rest or helping stabilise yourself for a clip, if the hold layout is appropriate. You need a couple of holds or, preferably, a foothold and a small overlap, such as the one shown in the photo (opposite top), that are approximately the same distance apart as the distance between your knee and foot.

With your foot on the lower hold, the knee

▲ Locking your leg between a foothold and an overlap or edge for your knee/thigh provides stability and rest

or thigh is wedged beneath the upper hold or lip. Standing up on your toes so your heel pushes upwards achieves the lock. Some holds can make this very uncomfortable, but a decent overlap or lip such as the one in the photo is ideal.

KNEE LOCK

A 'knee lock' is a technique for tackling cracks. If the crack is wide enough, place your knee into it until it wedges naturally, then flex your foot out of the crack and to the side to initiate the camming action that provides the lock. The other foot is positioned on whatever is available to provide a secondary brace. The crack width is critical. This technique can feel very insecure at first and may not be without pain. Trying it out at low level is strongly recommended, but it might be difficult to

find a good place to do that, as indoor walls are not always abounding in off-width cracks! You can also achieve a knee lock by lifting your heel once your knee is jammed – this expands the upper thigh and creates a lock. The crack width is critical. Rarely found indoors!

DYNO

Reaching up for the next handhold can be done in two general styles – 'static' and 'dynamic'.

▲ Nick Moulden demonstrates a 'static' reach. It takes great strength to be able to lock off on a small hold like this on a steep wall

⌃ Adam Lincoln demonstrates a 'dyno' – note his initial low, crouching position

- A 'static' move is a controlled reach. At the point at which you reach the target hold, you can maintain that position regardless of whether you grip the hold.
- A 'dynamic' move is one requiring some form of leap or jump. At the point at which you reach the target hold you are unable to maintain that position unless you grip the hold.

'Dynos' vary in exact style, but the standard dyno involves a dynamic leap from a set of hand- and footholds to reach a higher hold that could not be reached by a static move. To perform the move, the body is allowed to drop into a low position so that the arms are fully extended. This explosive move is then undertaken by pulling hard with the arms at the same time as you push upwards with your legs. As with all other powerful moves in other sports involving the whole body, timing and coordination are everything. The power output from your arms and legs has to be timed to perfection.

For the longest reaches, the leading exponents of the art continue the leg push right through into their toes, resulting in a jump from the best foothold, and the arm pull can be progressed right through to a dynamic push down with one hand, while the other hand reaches for the target hold. Top 'dynoists' will also swing their bodies below the start handholds to get a rhythm that they can carry through into the move.

One great leap

Just so that you realise how pathetic your dyno attempts really are, the farthest distance achieved in dyno competitions was 2.85m, set by Denver climber Skyler Weekes (height: 1.95m) on 3 July 2010, at the Cliffhanger Games/World Cup event in Sheffield. That's a long way!

There are many variations on dynos. Sometimes you can go for the 'target hold' with both hands, sometimes with one. The target hold may be more to one side or the other, and can require a slightly different set of movements. The more overhanging the wall on which you are attempting the dyno, the more you will be thrown out in the course of the move. It certainly takes a great deal of skill and practice to dyno successfully.

The American climber John Gill perfected the 'double dyno' many years ago and certainly ahead of his time – one dynamic move immediately followed by another.

Dynos are very common in indoor climbing and for many people may be the only way to complete a certain problem. You should be careful though, as performing dynos places huge stress on your fingers and shoulders in particular, and the move is a recognised source of injury problems.

▼ Dave Birkett dynoing for a high hold through an overhang

Short-range dynos

These are very common in indoor climbing. Holds that are within reach may still be better reached through a short-range dyno than statically. In modern bouldering it's very noticeable that many reaches that could be achieved statically are undertaken as short-range dynos. This style of climbing can usefully carry momentum through into the following move.

FOOT SWITCH

It's very common to have to change which foot you have on a given foothold. There are two common ways of doing this.

First is a standard 'share', in which the foot you're changing to shares the foothold and then takes over as you slide the first foot off. This is easy to do on big holds, but requires some skill to

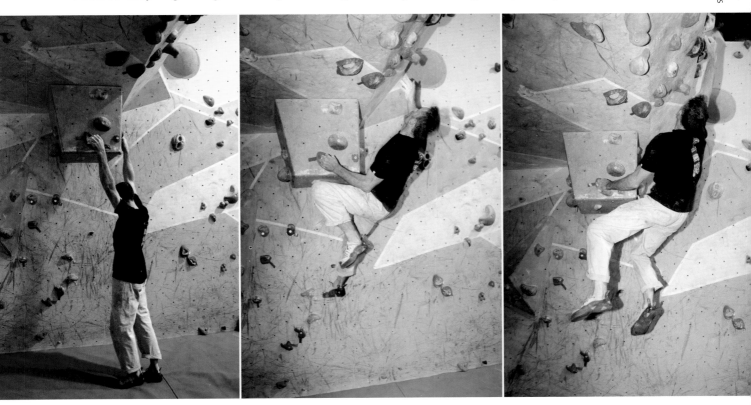

perform on small holds and may involve the new foot either pushing across from the side or standing on the tip of the foot on the hold temporarily before you slide the original foot out. It may help to temporarily friction the toe of the new foot on the wall above the existing foot, while you slip the original foot out. It's also common to temporarily unweight your existing foot to allow an easier change. Unweighting can be achieved by using your arms to unweight – or by a very slight jumping up action.

The second method of changing feet is to do a 'foot cross'. This is normally done in the following way. If your right foot is on the hold, your left foot crosses behind your right leg and shares the hold. Your right leg then pulls out of the hold and is moved across to the next one. Sometimes you may cross your foot on the inside, between the wall and your leg.

Foot switches are very common, and this is a technique you'll get plenty of opportunity to try, as many problems – especially traverses – require them in abundance.

CAMPUSING

This involves pulling up from hold to hold without using your feet. Campus boards provide a training routine with different-sized holds and with

◄ Note how the new foot is introduced sideways and over the top of the existing foot on a small hold such as this, before the existing foot is withdrawn

▼ Crossing behind or sometimes in front of your static foot is a common technique to allow a change in foot position

different vertical distances between the holds. In addition to using the technique as a training method, there are some instances where campusing is used as a method to overcome the lip of an overhang.

It may look pretty cool to do this, but in most situations you will want to use your feet as much as you can, either on holds under the overhang or by hooking around the lip, in order to conserve maximum arm strength.

There may be some cases, however, where the potential for using footholds is very limited and perhaps requires a very high level of body tension and core strength. In such cases, cutting loose and campusing through the overhang may be a better option. As always, it's the layout of the holds combined with your climbing style and reach that decides the best method.

◀ Dave Birkett making 'campusing' around an overhang look easy

▼ Adam Lincoln showing how body positions change, especially from the hips, during campus moves

LOCK OFF

A 'lock off' is simply holding the body in position with one hand – usually in a fully-bent-arm position, as you reach for a hold with the other. It's a static move. The steeper the wall, and the smaller the hold – the harder it is to lock off. All climbers use the lock off; it's one of the key climbing positions.

▲ Nick Moulden locking off with his right arm and reaching high

▲ A foot/hand match on a steep problem at The Arch, London

MATCH

If you match a hold, you're simply sharing hands on it – some people call it a 'share'. Often, one hand has a bigger share on the hold than the other and you may need to reposition your hands so that the other hand takes the biggest share to enable you to make the next move.

◄ A match (or 'share') at the top of a problem at The Arch, London

Hand/foot match

On harder moves involving high step-ups, you may have to retain a handhold while you place your foot on the same hold. This is relatively straightforward at slab angle, but when the wall is steep it requires a great deal of strength and flexibility.

FIGURE-OF-FOUR

After talking to several extremely good climbers about the figure-of-four move, I have only found one who had ever used one in anger. Although you do see a plethora of figure-of-four moves being practised by the dry toolers, it's a very unusual technique and one that the majority of climbers will never use.

However, if you're a potential contortionist with a penchant for the unusual and want to show off a bit, then here's how to do it. Let's say you've got both hands on and your right is on a really good hold. Start the figure of four by hooking your left leg over your right elbow joint. Then, shuffle your leg through until you can sit up high into a position in which you can reach up with your other hand. Sitting your leg on your elbow joint will allow a certain reach, but shuffle up to the wrist joint for a longer reach. If you haven't fallen off in a heap or injured yourself by now, well done.
Warning when trying this out, do so at a low level and use a partner to steady you and protect against falling. If you can make it work as a part of your repertoire of moves then good for you!

HEEL/TOE CAM

This involves locking your foot between two holds with your heel on the top of one hold and your toes beneath the other hold – your foot turned fully into the wall. Force can be applied by pulling upwards with the toes, which forces the heel down.

Toe cam in crack

Horizontal cracks are more common in outdoor climbing, but you'll find them at a few walls. Place your toe as deep into the crack as it will go and apply a torqueing action by pulling the toes up against the upper side of the crack. It's surprising how much force you can apply and it will help lock the position and reduce the effort expended through the arms. Watch that you don't get your foot stuck in the crack, though!

⌃ A heel/toe cam helps the climber to perform a difficult mantelshelf move

FOOT ROTATION

Many moves require 'foot rotation' through a hold. It's not difficult, but requires some focus to ensure that the best use is made of the hold throughout the rotation. Unless you have triple-jointed ankles, you'll find that your foot rotates about a foothold every time you alter your upper body position. Smaller body-position changes will result in smaller rotations. The ones that require some practice are when you're performing more dynamic moves in which the foot has to rotate through the hold at higher speed and with greater precision. It does happen quite naturally, but it's worth becoming aware of the type of movement and its relationship to your body positions. Foot rotation allows the climber to keep momentum through a move. You'll need to experiment with your exact foot position – dropping your heel slightly may make for an easier rotation.

ARM CROSS

An 'arm cross' is a simple move in which one arm crosses over the other on a traverse to allow the next holds to be reached more easily.

⌄ Nick Moulden demonstrating an arm cross

STEP THROUGH

The 'step through' is a very common technique in which one foot is crossed through the inside of the other leg onto the next foothold. This usually involves creating some space between your body and the wall/rock to allow the step through. It's particularly useful on traverses.

⌄ Adam Lincoln stepping through

REACH THROUGH

The reach through is the equivalent to the step through, but using the arms instead of the legs, as shown in the photo (opposite top). Note how the hips are locked in and the upper body has rotated through virtually 180 degrees and will do so again to come back to facing the wall after the next move. You can carry a lot of momentum through a move this way, but it needs to be carefully controlled.

▲ Nick Moulden performing a full reach through

CRACK CLIMBING

You don't get that many cracks on most climbing walls, but in outdoor climbing you'll come across crack climbs in abundance. Some people love crack climbing and some don't – you'll just have to try it out and see for yourself.

Thin cracks

To use thin finger cracks you adapt your 'finger-jamming' technique to the crack width. You can also finger jam in different hand positions – with either your forefinger or little finger facing down. The forefinger down position is more common.

In very narrow cracks you may just be able to insert your fingertips. In this case it is normal to turn your hand so that your forefinger is the lowest finger and rather like when you're feeling for the best place on a handhold, you're feeling for the best place to jam. It's then usual to push your fingers into the best place, then as you pull down on them, twist your hand back round into a more vertical position. This action has the effect of locking your fingers into the crack. There may be some pain! If the crack

is really thin you may have to do this with your little finger lowest.

In deeper cracks, simply insert your fingers until you find the position in which they most naturally lock, forefinger down, then twist your hand down again into a more vertical position to lock them.

Don't forget to remove rings and watches before tackling finger-jamming cracks.

▼ Andy Tilney climbing a thin finger crack – note how jams are often used in conjunction with layback moves

You'll find you may use your thumb to help, either by pulling up into the crack in a sort of pinch movement or by pressing sideways against the crack in what's called a 'thumb sprag'.

Finger jams are often used to pull sideways as well as downwards, turning the jam into a semi-layback.

▲ Finger jamming and a thumb sprag

Hand cracks

Wider cracks than finger width become 'hand cracks', requiring 'hand jamming'. Some people love hand jamming; many don't! I suspect of the many who don't like this technique that they simply don't know how to hand jam correctly, because when you do it right, it makes a fantastic hold.

To hand jam correctly, first relax your hand and let it slide into the crack in front of you, so that your fingers are vertical or just tilted a little into the crack. Move it up and down to see if you can feel a spot at which it feels like it will jam naturally. Next, slide your thumb into your palm and feel what happens to the base of your hand. It should have expanded. This expansion of the base of your hand is what provides most of the jamming action. Once you've done this, take your hand out and try again in a few different places, repeating the technique and feeling the most secure places.

▲ A classic example of jamming from Dave Birkett

⌄ A hand jam and foot jam are combined with a left-hand Gaston in order to climb this crack

Next, we're going to add some finger/hand tension. With your hand in the crack and your thumb slid into your palm to increase the hand base width, now press your fingers against the side of the crack and tense your fingers and hand in opposition to each other to maximize the jam. It should feel secure. It might hurt a bit as well, but persevere – it's a good pain!

You'll need to experiment with this technique as it takes a lot of practice to get it right and to deal with slightly different crack widths.

Most people get sore skin from hand jamming as a result of failing to jam securely enough and the hand then moving inside the crack when you pull on it. It's vital to find the most secure natural place within the crack to jam, then to lock in hard!

You can use a hand jam to layaway as an undercut hold and you can jam in both vertical and horizontal placements. This is a truly versatile hold once you've mastered it.

Fist crack

On cracks too wide for a hand jam you might need to go for a 'fist jam'. Once again find the point in the crack at which your fist naturally jams, this time with it in a front on rather than sideways position and clench your fist to expand your hand so the crack holds the outside of your little finger and the outside of the base of your thumb. This is fine if you have big, meaty builder's hands, but those with slender, well-manicured hands may shy away from this one!

Arm bar

In the unlikely event of an even wider crack (between conventional fist jamming width and chimney width) into which you can fit your arm, you can try an 'arm bar'. This involves turning side on to the crack and inserting your arm so that your hand is against one side and your elbow/upper arm against the other. Force your palm as hard as you can in opposition to your elbow/upper arm and feel the grip – or lack of it! To be used most effectively, an arm bar requires a lot of strength and confidence. If you have a suitable crack at your wall, do give it a try. An arm bar may be used in conjunction with another technique such as a Gaston.

This manoeuvre requires a little getting used to and may involve some minor discomfort – as occurs with finger and hand jamming. The exact technique used depends on the width of the crack.

Toe and foot jams

In the narrowest cracks, you may just be able to twist the very end of your toe in to get a hold. As

◄ Note how climber Andy Tilney is twisting his foot slightly to enter the crack. Straightening the foot prior to standing on it provides the locking jam.

the crack widens, you can twist your foot into a vertical position, place your toes into the crack and then twist your foot back to its normal position – which should provide you with a secure jam.

As the crack widens to take your whole foot, a convenient narrowing will sometimes offer a place to secure a great foot jam hold, but just a little wider and you may have to twist your foot so that one side of your heel pushes against one side of the crack, while the opposite side of your toes pushes against the other side. Tension applied through your foot and leg locks the foot in position through friction.

Off-width

This climbing technique is hard and involves strenuous techniques of wedging and shuffling. Masters of the off-width make it look easy. Everyone else struggles. Fortunately, for most of us off-widths are rare on indoor walls. Climbers the world over have developed their own specific techniques for off-width cracks. Perhaps the most famous is American Randy Leavitt's 'Leavittation' technique, which involves a combination of knee and leg jams in which the thigh muscles help jam your leg by expanding. This allows you to reach up and get a 'stacked' jam with your hands – jamming two limbs together, that is, two fist jams side by side. Look it up – it's impressive. Much depends on the width of the crack in relation to your hand, arms, knees and feet, though.

If you're lucky, the crack will widen and narrow during its length, allowing you to place your foot or toe at the point of narrowing, offering a more secure placement. The hardest toe and foot jams are in cracks that are parallel or that flare outwards the wrong way.

The final word about cracks is not to forget that you can use the edge of a crack to layback on and that sometimes the inside of the crack may have holds that you can use to pull on.

MAKE THE MOST OF IT – EXPERIMENT

In order to make the most of these techniques, you must experiment with them in numerous situations, on walls of different angles, with different hold layouts, and so on. Only when you have amassed a significant amount of experience will you start to automatically choose the right set of techniques for any given problem or route. Perform them often enough (several thousand times) and you'll develop the muscle memory and intuitive reactions which enable you to flow through moves requiring differing techniques smoothly and effectively.

Mastering advanced climbing techniques is a process that requires much practice, along with time to allow your body to develop the strength to be able to apply them correctly.

OTHER ADVANCED IDEAS FOR IMPROVING YOUR CLIMBING LEVEL

Downclimbing

Most people don't 'downclimb', but it has a couple of advantages. First, your muscles are being used in a different way to the way in which you used them going up, which is good for overall equalisation of muscle development and injury prevention. Second, it is a good skill to learn if you want to climb outside on real rock at some point, where it's common to have to reverse-climb a move – back to a resting place, for example, while you work out the next move.

Generating momentum

The generation and maintenance of momentum is often the key to steep and difficult sections of climbing.

Many climbers are brought up on a diet of lead climbing on outdoor rock climb in a very static and controlled manner, which suits their type of climbing. Leaping into the unknown for holds on which you may or may not be able to hang isn't such an attractive idea when your last piece of protection is a small wire several metres below you!

On indoor walls there is a greater degree of certainty and higher levels of safety. This allows climbers to use momentum in a series of moves to better effect. Many techniques and factors combine to allow you to use momentum. Usually generated by the lower part of the body, momentum is then often increased through pulling or pushing with the upper body. Dynamic moves combined with changes in body position and foot rotations offer the possibility of carrying momentum forwards into the next move.

Think about it – if your body is pulled up and then stops, you need to apply a significant force to get it moving again. If you can use the momentum generated from the move and carry it forward into the next move without stopping, it's a much more efficient way of using your energy. You can generate momentum on any angle of rock – it works on slabs just the same as on overhanging walls.

One great example of carrying momentum through into another move is the double dyno, perfected originally by American bouldering legend John Gill. Search for this on the internet – it's well worth a look.

Resting

There is a real art to this one. Although a 'resting' position for a lead climber might be an impossible position for a beginner to even to get into, the principle remains the same at all standards. If you find a place to stop at in which you are able to recover rather than continue depleting your strength, it's a resting place.

The best and easiest resting positions involve bridging – pushing the feet in opposition to each other, usually in a corner – to support your weight without the use of handholds. Large, conveniently spaced footholds create easy bridging and an easy rest. You'll need more technique and higher levels of flexibility to use smaller and more widely spaced bridging footholds.

Chimneying positions also allow resting. Your feet push against a wall while your upper body is wedged against an opposing one. You could also rest your upper body against a volume or even the edge of a crack. The common ground between this and the bridging position is that it uses opposing forces.

Other resting positions may involve the use of a toe or heel hook around an edge or hold or simply the repositioning of feet and hands to find the least stressful place to stop. Holding on with your arms straight and as relaxed as possible provides the best opportunity for rest.

It's well worth practising this very deliberately on routes. Stop in random places and try to find a resting position. Vary the angle and type of climb. You'll also find this very useful for learning how to find the best positions from which to clip when you're lead climbing.

◄ A bridging position can bring a welcome rest, even on small footholds

▲ Resting alternate arms on a steep wall often means finding a relaxed position and straight-arm hanging

Clipping positions

Rather like finding positions in which you can rest, in order to clip cleanly and safely you want to distribute as much weight as possible to your feet and be in as balanced a position as possible. This will allow you to take one hand off to clip.

Here are a few ideas to work on for making your clipping as easy as possible:

Straight-arm or dead hang If the position allows, keep your arm straight and just hang from the hold. Don't grip too hard; just relax. Straight-arm hangs use less of your precious strength. If you need to pull in to clip, do so when you are ready as the bent-arm position weakens you faster.

Focus on your feet Sorting your feet out so that they can take the maximum amount of weight while you clip is essential. The best clipping position might not be the best climbing position. If the crucial footholds are high, you may have to adopt

▲ A straight-arm clip from a relaxed position

one of the techniques previously mentioned to get your hips pulled in and get more weight to your feet.

Centre of gravity Try to position yourself so your centre of gravity is as far as possible over your feet and use your arms simply to hold the position. If your feet are off to one side, you'll need to use more strength in your upper body to maintain the position.

Practise Try lots of different clipping positions on easier routes until you start to find the best position as a matter of course.

While practising positional technique, also practise clipping quickdraws from different angles: left, right, above, below, diagonal.

Note Remember that you must take into account other clipping factors such as how near the ground you are and the potential consequences of falling, while in the process of clipping.

Overhangs and roof climbing

An 'overhang' is the term used to describe the wall when it turns at a large angle away from the vertical – usually about 90 degrees. An overhang may be very small – sometimes just a third of a metre or so, when it is often called an 'overlap'. A really big overhang – perhaps a body length or greater, becomes a 'roof'. When you're climbing a roof or an overhang, your weight is predominantly on your arms, which clearly tire faster than your legs. However, making good use of your feet is critical in helping reduce the amount of weight your arms have to take, and they are often used in quite imaginative ways.

Toe and heel hooks are very common; flagging and twist locks also. 'Toe cams', where your toe pulls

⌄ A sequence showing the ascent of a large roof at the Redpoint Climbing Centre, Birmingham. Note the many different body positions adopted during the climb

upwards into the roof, or 'heel/toe cams', between the roof and a hold or between two holds, may also help.

You'll find that you're changing your body position frequently to take advantage of the full range of holds on offer (see the roof climbing sequence on the previous page).

Strong stomach muscles and good core strength help to maintain the body positions required. **Note** It's usually best to keep your arms straight as much as possible. This allows longer movements and the position uses less strength.

Reading the route and visualisation

You'll often see climbers at the foot of a route or problem, standing back a little and moving their hands about while gazing intently at the route as if in a trance. You'd be forgiven for thinking this was some sort of bizarre ritual, but working out the route in advance is actually really useful, and the more experience you have, the more accurately you can predict the moves.

'Reading the route' like this involves identifying key holds and their positions, the angle of the wall and the types of move you'll be likely to make. You can also identify potential resting positions.

'Visualisation' takes this process a stage further, by taking the reading of the route and converting it into a feeling. While reading a route produces a series of information, visualisation takes this information and applies it in a stronger way.

Visualisation techniques are well-documented and are used by most professional athletes. Techniques may involve imagining watching yourself doing the route, through to a stage where you're feeling the holds, the moves and the body movements in an extremely vivid, yet imaginary way. Some athletes describe the visualisation process as so intense that when performing a task, they feel like they have done it before.

How far you want to take this mental approach to climbing is very much up to you as an individual. I've found that reading routes in a logical and planned way really helps prepare you for the climb, but for boulder problems in particular or for specific hard moves, more intense visualisation techniques are extremely valuable.

You'll just have to try it and see what works for you. There are many references to visualisation techniques on the internet and in sports training books.

▲ Intense concentration allows you to visualise the route or problem

▲ 'Taking a whipper' at Kendal Wall

Falling off

Do you really need to train to fall off? Some people do, but it has to be done in a very controlled fashion and with a very clear purpose in mind. If you're scared to fall off and you won't push yourself hard enough to take the occasional 'lob', this could be holding back your development as a climber. In such cases, arranging a few progressive falls from a slump on the rope through to a short but meaningful fall can give you the confidence to try those harder routes without the background fear of falling and without you feeling the need to grab the nearest quickdraw at the first signs of fatigue! This is best done with a very experienced partner or an instructor, who can make sure the falls are controlled and take place on a high section of wall, set at an angle, on which you're unlikely to hurt yourself.

SUMMARY
Select the right technique
Good technique enables you to climb more and to climb harder. Anyone can go to a wall and learn how to undertake a certain technique, but the key skill is in selecting the right technique to use on any given route or problem.

Experiment
The only way you are going to do this is to experiment. Try using the different techniques on different types of route – slabs, overhanging walls, vertical routes, corners, and so on. Only by experimenting will you build up the knowledge and confidence that will allow you to select the right technique.

Work on your weaknesses – turn them into strengths
Identify your weaknesses. While you're trying these techniques out you'll find you favour some over others. You'll quickly become a master of certain techniques, while others will remain part of your 'hidden repertoire' (that is, the ones you're not very good at). By all means enjoy the moves you're good at, but do work on your weaknesses – eventually you may turn them into another strength.

Watch and learn
Watch other climbers. Some climbers make difficult moves look so easy. What is it that makes this happen? Focus on their technique and style. Are they more flexible than you? Stronger? Are they using a certain technique better than you can? You can learn a lot from watching other, better climbers – always be prepared to learn.

8

TRAINING TO IMPROVE YOUR CLIMBING

with help from Adrain Baxter
of ClimbCoach, Dave Birkett,
Nick Moulden and Adam Lincoln

This section deals with improving your climbing standard through training and describes the training principles adopted by some climbers. What works for one person may not work as well for another, so it's important that you find a training programme that suits your fitness level, your commitment and your lifestyle.

You should remember that training can take many guises and need not involve a gym. For many people new to climbing, initial gains can be made very successfully by concentrating on technique,

⌄ Enjoy lots of climbing and concentrate on technique to start with

⌃ Quick gains can be made in your flexibility – an ideal goal for new climbers and crucial for more advanced climbing

enjoying lots of achievable routes and boulder problems, and improving flexibility. Many coaches recommend newcomers to climbing spend months or even years developing technique and developing the very specific strengths required for the sport before starting to train seriously.

To improve your climbing standard you can apply several straightforward basic principles:

- Increase your strength.
- Improve your power.
- Improve your endurance.
- Improve your flexibility.
- Improve your technique.
- Improve your mental approach.
- Lose your weight.

In your first months of climbing you should focus on the last four on the list, and enjoy lots of routes and bouldering.

THE 'NATURAL' CLIMBER

I am not a climbing natural, and only managed to climb to a half decent standard by training. Indoor walls formed an important part of that training. How I envied some of my peers! Climbers such as Pat McVeigh seemed to have such a natural ability to climb. You could tell by watching Pat for a while that much of his skill came naturally and not from hard hours of training. Some people just have that gift. If – like me – you don't, then you have to work extremely hard.

My first climbing experience was with the founder of Wild Country, Mark Vallance. I was working in the Peak District National Park in the mid-1970s and Mark, who had just returned from Yosemite, volunteered to take me climbing. I turned up in a pair of big mountain boots and variously climbed and was pulled up some classic routes at Millstone Edge, South Yorkshire, including The Mall and Bond Street. I was hooked.

My climbing 'apprenticeship' then took place amongst Yorkshire's gritstone outcrops, primarily Almscliffe, Brimham, Ilkley and Caley. We climbed all year, in all weathers. I recall my hands freezing tight to the metal bar across the top of the climb Lover's Leap at Brimham – and anxious moments on footholds as slippery as soap as the autumn mists dampened the rock. The VS grade seemed so far distant as to be almost an illusion. I genuinely thought that I would never be able to lead climb at VS standard. I persevered with dozens of Diffs and V Diffs, and moved on to Severe grade climbs. I climbed long routes in North Wales and the Lakes and then discovered climbing walls. The Leeds Wall, a corridor of polished brickwork and even more polished rock edges, proved a bit too intense to start with so we found a new wall at Rothwell, the original, complete with concrete jamming pods, a concrete slab, a short overhanging wall with a capping roof and a great low-level traverse.

I trained on the wall with no set plan and with no technical knowledge of training. I simply did lots of traverses mixed up with short strenuous problems and some solo climbing, which gradually drew me into higher and more precarious places on the wall. I enjoyed the experience of informal competition with my friends, the exercise and the feeling of improvement.

The following year I led my first E1 – North Crag Eliminate at Castle Rock – and the new levels of fitness that training on the indoor wall had provided enabled me to crack the Extreme grades that I had thought previously unattainable. Even the solo climbing on the wall helped, by giving me the confidence to climb above protection.

The next big improvement in climbing for me arrived with the development of the Ambleside Climbing Wall. I increased my leading grade from E1 to E3/4 simply by training on the Ambleside Wall. Circuits on the overhanging wall, traverses and the Bachar ladder all helped.

The problem for me though was that it was all a bit like advertising must be for a big company. You do lots of it and some of it works, but you're not entirely certain which bits.

The things that improved my climbing grade
- Lots of bouldering.
- Interval training on a climbing wall.
- Regularly soloing routes.
- Losing weight.

That was all very amateurish and I was fortunate that several years of climbing lots of routes outside had allowed my key muscles, ligaments and tendons to develop the strength required for training.

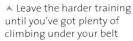 Leave the harder training until you've got plenty of climbing under your belt

∧ You can lower the difficulty of pull-ups by using bigger holds and putting your feet on something to share your weight – varying the position of the 'foot holds' will alter the difficulty of the pull-up

AN INTRODUCTION TO TRAINING

Training nowadays at the higher levels of all sports is very scientific, very focused and very specific. You'll be able to discover regimes designed by leading athletes and climbers in books and through the internet. The latest developments include a range of apps for training such as ClimbCoach by Steve McClure and Adrian Baxter, who also contributed this section. The availability of such easy-to-use and functional training regimes leaves you with no excuses.

Do I really need to 'train'?

If your aspirations are to get physically stronger or fitter in an attempt to fast-forward yourself through the grades – starting to train probably is the answer.

Especially when starting out with climbing training, simply committing yourself to visiting the wall reasonably regularly, setting yourself a goal and working a weakness each time you climb is enough to make a big difference to your ability.

When is the right time to start training?

Learn how to climb before learning how to train. This is for two reasons. First, climbing is a very technical sport: it takes years to master the basics of movement, balance and efficiency. Within the first two to three years of climbing any significant gain in strength will probably not match the potential total performance gain that can be made through just climbing and improving technique.

Second, climbing and bouldering put exceptional strain on very specific and delicate muscle and tendon groups (mainly in the fingers and forearms) that are highly prone to injury. Therefore, physiologically 'easing' these muscle groups into climbing and strengthening them slowly and safely over a two-year period is time well invested. Injuries are easy to pick up early in a climbing career, but very hard to lose.

What should I train on?

Keep it simple. Boulder problems, routes and a pull-bar are all you need for a really effective training session:

- Use boulder problems to improve maximum strength and power.
- Use routes to improve resistance and endurance.
- A pull-up bar will help not just upper body strength through doing pull-ups, but also helps increase core strength through doing exercises like leg-raises and points. Powerundercut

⌄ Bouldering is great for improving maximum strength and power

➤ Long routes are perfect for improving resistance and endurance

▲ Training for power on a boulder problem

Keep away from most things wooden and metal. That means campus boards, fingerboards and weights are out of the question, if you are just starting out with training. There is no question that they are effective training tools, but only when you've a few years' climbing experience under your belt.

The 3 S's of training

KEEP IT SIMPLE

Choose one motivating and realistic goal.

Work out the one thing that is holding you back from achieving that goal.

Commit some time every climbing session to training that one weakness.

KEEP IT SOCIABLE

Ben & Jerry, Yuji & Francois, Tommy & Kevin … There's little wonder why the greatest things in climbing have been achieved by climbing partners.

Keeping training 'sociable' is really about keeping it fun. You'll not only be more likely to turn up to train if your friends are there, but a healthy sense of competition between you and your friends will also keep you motivated during training.

KEEP IT SAFE

There's a fine line between pushing yourself safely during training and pushing yourself too far. One of the best pieces of advice I was given was to leave each training session with something left to give and to never, never leave one exhausted.

It will take you much longer to recover between sessions if you are exhausted (meaning you'll actually end up doing less training sessions in the long term) and you're also much more likely to overtrain and pick up an injury, if you train when tired.

Top training tips

GOALS

Always have a goal. If you don't, what are you training for? Goals make training motivating as you see where you're aiming and how close you are to getting there. Make goals as specific and realistic as possible.

FOCUS

Focus your training time into blocks of specific workouts. For example, six weeks of maximum strength, followed by six weeks of resistance. Don't train too many things at once; it will result in you not being very good at everything.

TRAINING ORDER

Always train the more strength-based fitness aspects first; that is, maximum strength, then power, then resistance, then endurance. This applies to any time period of training, whether a month, a week or a day. If you don't, the quality of your session will be compromised and you're more likely to get injured.

CONSISTENCY

Consistency is king. You'll reach your goals much quicker if you are regular with your training. The body is very good at learning and adapting when we do something consistently.

VARIATION

If you only train the same thing, you'll only be good at that thing! Although it's important to be consistent with your training, it's equally important to vary the way that you train in order to keep the body guessing and constantly adapting.

REST

Rest is as important as training. Without sufficient rest, you can't recover and, consequently, you'll not get as fit or strong as quickly as you could. So, if you feel tired prior to training or have any aches or pains, you haven't rested enough … so don't train!

AVOIDING INJURY

Always err on the safe side of training. When you are going well it's always a temptation to push a bit harder. However, the harder you push towards your limits the more likely you are to get injured. Never train if you feel tired, are sore or have aches and pains from your last session.

Training terminology and guidelines

MAXIMUM STRENGTH

What it is 'The greatest force that is possible to exert in a single contraction'. In climbing, it's the ability to hold onto a very small hold or to perform a body movement in a certain direction, for example, a single pull-up.

Why it's important Without good maximum strength you won't be able to hold onto a hold or make a particular strength-based move. Without being able to do this you will obviously then not be able to complete a route or boulder problem.

Equipment to use Stick to boulder problems (keep away from campus and fingerboards until you've had at least three years' regular climbing experience).

Training frequency Two to three (maximum) times per week.

Rest between sessions At least 72 hours.

Training phase length Three to five weeks maximum.

POWER

What it is 'The rate of producing force in a certain direction'. In climbing, it's the ability to make moves between holds or move your body between positions.

Why it's important Without good power levels, you literally won't be able make powerful or dynamic moves between holds.

Equipment to use Again, stick to boulder problems only until you've had a few years' experience.

Training frequency Two to three (maximum) times per week.

Rest between sessions At least 72 hours.

Training phase length Three to five weeks maximum.

RESISTANCE

What it is 'The ability to make a continual set of contractions (moves) or to hold holds'. In climbing, this usually results in fatiguing the forearms by the creation of lactic acid (a pump) that a climber's body will need to try to eliminate or recover from in order to continue climbing. **Note**: resistance has many synonyms including 'power endurance', 'strength endurance', 'medium duration muscular endurance' and 'anaerobic capacity'.

Why it's important Good resistance fitness levels are the key to success on routes. Often individual moves on routes are not that hard, but it is the succession of them that makes a route hard to climb. Having good resistance fitness levels means that you can better cope with these successions of moves without tiring.

Equipment to use Routes and circuits are best for increasing resistance levels as they allow you to link together successions of moves. Boulder problems can also be linked together to achieve the same effect.

Training frequency Two to three times per week.

Rest between sessions 48 to 72 hours.

Training phase length Eight to ten weeks maximum (with a rest week after every fourth week).

ENDURANCE

What it is 'Low-intensity, high-volume aerobic exercise'.

Why it's important Endurance training should make up a significant base of any route climber's training schedule. It will both aid quicker recovery between routes and allow climbers to climb for longer, especially on long days out or multipitch routes.

Training frequency Three to four times per week.

Rest between sessions (Beginner) 24 to 48 hours.

Training phase length Eight to ten weeks maximum (with a rest week after every fourth week).

TRAINING – THE PROS

Dave Birkett

Of course there are other, less scientific methods of training. Take Lakeland climber Dave Birkett. Much of Dave's training as a young lad was based on hard days on the fells shepherding with his grandfather and the hard-work theme didn't stop there. Although Dave has undergone periods of more

▲ Legendary Lakes' climber Dave Birkett

conventional training, much of his climbing fitness has been developed through bouldering and a large quantity of climbing, coupled with lots of hard work in his job as a stonemason and dry-stone waller. Dave says:

> When I was doing my hardest routes, I trained for specific moves by replicating them. If I was doing a very powerful move off an undercut, I would do curls and so on to develop that particular type of specific strength. I found the gains to be quite quick.

▲ Circuits on a bouldering wall at an appropriately easy grade provide good endurance training

This type of training is well-documented – climbers have trained for cracks and for specific moves by building copies of the actual move, and working on it repeatedly. Move-specific or even route-specific training is great when you're struggling with one particular move or technique.

RECOVERING FROM INJURY

Dave's earlier climbing days were disrupted following a bad knee injury, not helped when he damaged the knee again after the first cast was removed. He spent almost eight months in a cast, but Dave used this non-climbing period to develop his upper body strength. Dave recalls:

> I could do three one-finger pull-ups and was very strong, but I got really pumped on an E2 when I started climbing again – I hadn't had chance to apply the strength to my climbing.

This kick-started Dave's phenomenal climbing career and acted as a springboard from which to transfer the strength he'd developed into his climbing.

USING THE DAY JOB

Dave reckons his work as a stonemason has helped too.

> I don't have any sort of set training at work, but I might do some presses with bags of cement or curls with buckets of water. I think hard physical work has helped me maintain a steady standard through the years. Lots of climbers have peaks and troughs, but I've tended to maintain a standard most of the time. If I'm working on scaffolding I'll climb up and down that rather than use the ladders, and do pull-ups on it. It's not scientific.

There's little doubt that physical work helps with overall fitness and core strength and it's likely that it also helps to avoid injury in climbing.

With no formal training regime, coach or detailed knowledge of modern training and nutrition methods, Dave still managed to climb some extraordinarily hard routes, so does he think a formal coaching programme would have enabled him to climb even harder?

Yes, when 8c was the highest grade in climbing, I'd done pretty much all the 8bs in this country without having any sort of coaching or proper training. It's important to be able to convert your strength into climbing ability and I've always been able to do that, so if I'd been stronger I could have climbed harder routes.

So does Dave train at climbing walls?

I do use climbing walls, but don't tend to try too hard, it's more of a social thing. I do go to my mate's barn to do some training. Usually a warm-up followed by circuits and traverses on a bouldering wall, pull-ups, sit-ups and hangs. I find it easier to train hard when I'm on my own.

MENTAL PREPARATION

Dave's well-known for the serious and bold nature of the climbing on many of his first ascents, so how does he prepare himself mentally for them?

I visualise everything and go through it all time and time and again. Once I've worked on a route and visualised it so many times, I know I can climb it. You get to a point in your mind where the route's already done. The game's won when you know you can do it even before the ascent. When I get to the route, I just see how it feels and I know in the first couple of moves if it's going

to go. When Jerry Moffat won the Leeds competition years ago he used to visualise everything from walking on to the stage, putting his harness on and tying in, waving to the crowd – absolutely everything.

I agree completely with Dave about this – no matter what standard you're climbing at, using visualisation and other aspects of physical training will enable you to get to a stage where your confidence level is very high – so high that you know you can do it. It's the same thing when you've been trying a boulder problem for a long time. Once you've done it you know that you can do it, so can usually repeat it time after time.

LEARNING FROM EXPERIENCE

So what's Dave learnt about training as he's got a bit older?

One of the big things I've leaned as I've got older is to know how important resting is. One of the top South African climbers I know used to train hard until two weeks before a competition and then stop, just doing a bit of light exercise immediately before the event. It's really important to work on your weaknesses and you can turn them into strengths. After bouldering now I usually try to drink a chocolate milkshake straight afterwards!

Dave's methods wouldn't suit everybody, but what particularly interested me was how he integrates training with his job – there's a principle here that your training has to reflect the time you have available and the lifestyle you lead – and how important the mental aspect of visualisation is to him.

Nick Moulden

A current member of the British lead climbing team, Nick Moulden was kind enough to share some of his thoughts on training with me. As a competitive climber, Nick has a coach to help him train and it was clear talking to Nick that coaches have different views on how to increase performance. Simply changing coach, and therefore training style, has given Nick some significant improvements.

A typical training session always involves a serious warm-up and the training itself involves circuits on bouldering walls and number boards alongside interval training on routes. He describes how important it is to apply your training methods to the desired end result – in Nick's case, leading routes rather than bouldering is the priority. He also structures his training in order to peak at competition times, ensuring that there are sufficient rest periods built into his schedule.

In the winter months Nick goes to Malham in North Yorkshire to climb by head torch, just to get some mileage in on real rock, a point that highlights one of the key personal requirements as far as training is concerned – enthusiasm combined with commitment.

▼ Nick Moulden doing pull-ups on small, two-finger holds. You need to be very strong and have sufficient experience to do this without risk of injury.

Adam Lincoln

Adam Lincoln is another Evolv-sponsored climber, who operates at a very high level. With a more relaxed attitude to warming up than Nick Moulden, Adam's training is a direct reflection of the type of climbing he expects to be doing in the coming period, whether long continental sport climbs or shorter climbing wall routes.

Adam believes that 'pretty much anybody can climb 8a'.

I thought about that for a while and although I don't agree totally, his general point that most people could reach a good level of climbing standard through hard work and training is quite right. If he'd said 7a I might have agreed with him!

Here's a summary of Adam's key pointers for training:

- Work on weaknesses and be aware that they can develop into strengths and vice-versa.
- Have a seasonal approach to your climbing, working towards set goals.
- If you reach a plateau, consider other factors outside training for climbing to break through to the next level. These could include nutrition, coaching and cross training.
- Warm-ups involve some stretching, but more aerobic activity such as skipping, running and using Therabands. Use easier routes as warm-ups.
- As you become more experienced you'll know when in your warm-up you're ready to start climbing.
- Vary your training so your body doesn't get used to the same thing.
- Have specific goals to focus your training.
- Make sure you drink plenty so you're well-hydrated during training and climbing and drink a protein shake within 45 minutes of the end of your training session.
- Concentrate on technique and become really efficient as a climber.

▲ Adam Lincoln demonstrating a typical warm-up session involving an aerobic activity to raise heart rate – Theraband stretching, upper-body looseners, dead hangs, finger/forearm stretches and lower-standard bouldering

NUTRITION

In addition to training for the fundamental techniques and fitness required for climbing, improvements can be found by looking at your nutrition and developing your mental approach to climbing.

Many years ago I remember a climber weighing her food out very precisely in order to give herself a balanced diet (pun intended!). In contrast, my climbing partner, Wilf, and I made and consumed huge 'pork outs' of chilli, liver and mash and pretty much anything else you can think of. She was ahead of her time and doing the right thing. We were just greedy! There's a huge amount of information available on sports nutrition, but this summary is specifically related to climbing.

Sport climbing may not burn as many calories as running or cycling, but the energy expended tends to be concentrated through a specific set of muscles.

Muscles have two sources of energy – 'aerobic', in which ATP (adenosine triphosphate) is generated in the presence of oxygen, and 'anaerobic', in which ATP is produced without oxygen. Sustained contraction of the forearm – one of the key movements in climbing – relies almost exclusively on the anaerobic system, which is massively less efficient than the aerobic one. The result is that your muscles tire quicker and nutrient stores that produce energy are depleted more rapidly. As if that isn't enough, lactic acid build-up, which has a high correlation with fatigue, is faster. What you eat and when you eat it is critical to both your current training/climbing session and your ability to recover well for the next one.

Nutritional advice to help you climb better for longer falls into three general categories – pre-climb, during climbing/training and recovery.

Pre-climb key points

- Dehydration significantly impairs muscle performance, so hydrate fully: water is best.
- Muscle energy is stored in the form of glycogen, which comes from carbohydrates. Though the muscle stores of glycogen deplete rapidly, it can be replenished from blood glucose. The aim is, therefore, to raise blood glucose levels before climbing. Different forms of carbohydrate will release energy at different rates. Slow burn – or low GI carbs – will work best, eaten two to four hours before climbing or training. The food you ate yesterday will help fuel your muscles.
- Protein is also important. Linked with improving rehydration, it also helps reduce the levels of signals of fatigue coming from the brain. These signals contribute to muscle fatigue.

During climbing and training points

- Keep hydrated by drinking water frequently.
- Use quick release high-energy foods to maintain blood glucose levels. Examples would be raisins, chocolate or bananas. Between 30 and 60g per hour is recommended.

- Use a carb/protein shake/gel. Some research indicated a 56 per cent reduction in muscle damage compared to a standard carb only, drink. A 1:4 carbohydrate/protein mix is recommended.

Recovery pointers

- Rehydration is very important following climbing and this often takes place at the pub.
- However, it's recommended by experts that you eat to recover before you enjoy your hard-earned beer. It's recognised that during the 45-minute period following exercise, the mechanisms responsible for replenishing energy stores, rebuilding muscle protein and reducing muscle damage work at a heightened state. The right combination of nutrients will help you recover faster and perform better next time.
- A 4:1 carbohydrate /protein mix is ideal for this.
- Remember that children and young people taking part in climbing and training sessions will require more food than adults, as they are supplying nourishment for a growing body as well as training needs.

For further information from Adrian Baxter see www.climbcoach.org

9

ACCIDENT PREVENTION

I've spent over 35 years as an active climber and mountaineer. I've also enjoyed paragliding, skiing – off-piste, on-piste and wind-assisted – and many other mountain sports. I've been involved in mountain rescue and have come across many accidents over the years simply by chance. The one thing that has always stood out to me is that the time you're most likely to have an accident is when you perceive that the levels of risk are low.

Indoor climbing seems, on first acquaintance, to be quite a low-risk activity, and the easy-access, benign indoor environment and sheer number of other people climbing tend to amplify this.

However, indoor climbing carries many risks. Sure, you don't have to contend with falling rocks and ice, avalanches or crevasses, unusual and the descent doesn't normally involve a death-defying, slime- and moss-encrusted gully. But the ground is still usually hard and still hurts when you fall.

▲ You need to take extra care in a busy climbing wall environment

Although accidents will always happen, we can learn from previous incidents and near misses and try to make sure that similar circumstances don't conspire to catch us out again. Indoor climbing accidents can be broadly broken down into the following categories:

- Misuse of equipment.
- Failure of equipment.
- Falling climber on rope.
- Falling climber bouldering.

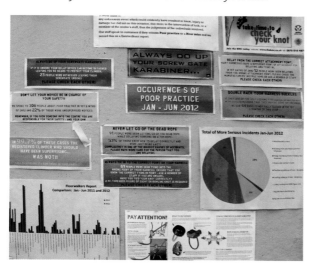

◄ The incident advisory board at The Castle Climbing Centre – a great way to drive home the message about accident prevention

Some accidents may be connected to more than one category, and other freak accidents also may occur, but it still provides a useful framework.

I spent an enjoyable afternoon at The Castle Climbing Centre and came across a notice board jam-packed with information regarding accidents and near misses. It made interesting reading, and established the point that most accidents are a result of lack of basic knowledge, distraction or over-familiarity. Experienced climbers appeared to be just as much at risk as beginners. Here's a summary of some of the main problem areas.

MISUSE OF EQUIPMENT

Harness

▲ An incorrectly fastened buckle: make sure your waistbelt buckle has not been left unlocked, like this one

BUCKLE
An incorrectly fastened buckle can cause your harness to come undone.
Solution Don't get distracted when you're fastening your buckles – finish the job and get your climbing partner to check it before you climb.

FITTING
It's not uncommon to see harnesses fitted incorrectly – for example, a leg loop or the belay loop twisted. These problems on their own are not going to cause your harness to fail, but they could lead to other problems, so always ensure your harness is aligned correctly. Check other harness features such as the straps at the back holding the leg loops up and make sure they are not slack or undone. If they are, it might allow the leg loops to slide down at the back and this could turn you upside down in the event of a fall.
Solution Make sure you know how to put your harness on correctly and check it.

BELAY AND TIE-IN POINTS
It is possible to clip your belay carabiner or tie on to the wrong point on your harness. The ones to watch out for are the gear loops and the small strap that holds the leg loops in position, both of which would be extremely unsafe to use. It is possible to clip the belay plate to other, structurally sound parts of the harness, but not as per manufacturers' instructions. The waist belt would be an example of this.
Solution Double check/buddy check that your tie-in and belaying points are being used correctly.

⌄ Twisted leg loops – a slack or unfastened rear strap could mean turning upside down in the event of a fall

LOOSE WAISTBELT

A loose waistbelt is sometimes seen on children, but can also be found on adult climbers. This occurs for three main reasons. First, the tension was not correct at the start or when the harness was put back on following removal. Second, the climber removed bulky clothing that was in place when

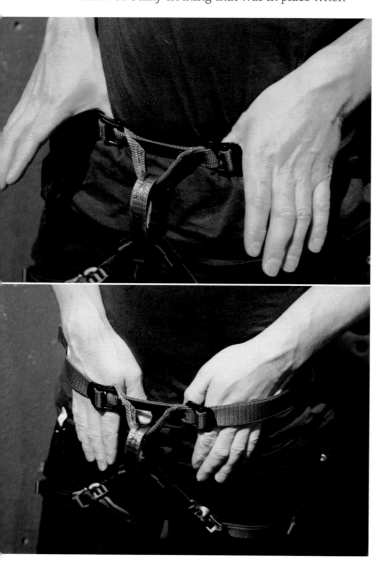

▲ Tension check – two thumbs down the front of your waistbelt is fine, but not two hands!

the harness was fitted; and third, the quick-fasten buckle has been interfered with accidentally, resulting in it slackening. A loose waistbelt can cause the harness to slip down and become positioned lower on the body than should be the case. In some adults, especially those who have been downing too much ale and eating too many pies, it is possible to fit the harness correctly initially at a true waist level, only for the harness to slip down to hip level and feel looser due to the body shape. This can cause a climber of any age to fall upside down as the centre of gravity becomes much higher than the actual attachment point..

Solution Ensure the correct fitting of the harness at the outset, and check the tension frequently – especially if you are supervising others.

Tying into your harness

KNOT FAILURE

Knot failure at the harness is extremely rare, but can clearly be catastrophic. It has been known to happen with bowlines tied incorrectly and with knots started, but not finished. Many incorrectly tied figure-of-eight knots will hold.

One of the main problems with knot tying is distraction and the speed of turnaround from one climber to another. If you're top roping, as soon as one climber is lowered down, another is often tying on, and it only takes a little distraction for a mistake to be made. I have seen for myself, on several occasions, experienced climbers getting ready to climb not having tied in correctly, and in one case not even having tied in at all. Each time the final check made before setting off on the climb highlighted the problem.

Solution Learn to tie a figure-of-eight knot correctly and don't climb until you and your climbing partner have checked it. If you use a bowline, ensure it's tied correctly and locked off – perhaps better still, use a figure-of-eight.

▲ Check your knot before climbing. A figure-of-eight knot correctly tied should have a double rope on every part of the knot. This one is wrong – it's an easy check to make

➤ Get your partner to check your knot and tie-in point

CARABINER CLIP-IN

Some people still clip in with a carabiner fastened to the belay loop and secured to the rope with a figure-of-eight knot on the bight. This is particularly common with some groups and is to be discouraged. It is against the rules of many climbing walls. The carabiner is an extra and unnecessary link in the chain – another thing that can go wrong. It is normally used simply because it is easier and quicker than tying and untying figure-of-eight knots. What can go wrong? The carabiner can be left with the gate unlocked or, indeed, in some circumstances could come undone on the climb, which in turn could lead to the rope unhitching from the carabiner and a complete detachment of the rope from the climber. And inexperienced users could easily clip the carabiner to the wrong point on the harness.

Solution Easy – don't be lazy. Tie in with a figure-of-eight knot.

▲ Tie in with a figure-of-eight knot

Misuse of belay device/ poor belaying

GATE LOCKING

The gate on a carabiner used for belaying must be of the locking type. The gate must be locked prior to use to prevent the accidental release of the rope from the carabiner. Though this is unlikely to happen, the consequences are potentially very serious. If the gate is undone, the carabiner can also fail at relatively low loading – it may have less than a third of its strength than in a locked position.

▲ Gate open/gate closed – there's not much difference at first glance. This Petzl carabiner has a red marking to warn you if the gate has left open.

▲ Try to push the gate open to ensure it's locked

Solution Always lock the gate as part of the process of preparing to belay someone. Perform a quick check prior to the climb: use your hand to try to push the gate open. Beginners should get their partner to check this.

CARABINER CROSS-LOADING

The belay carabiner can revolve around its attachment point, and can get into a position where the rope to belay loop loading is transferred across

▼ A cross-loaded carabiner

the width of the carabiner, rather than along its length. This reduces its breaking force by more than two-thirds and is potentially dangerous.

Solution Use a carabiner with a plastic clip that is fastened across to prevent rotation, or a combination of belay device and carabiner designed to prevent cross-loading, such as the Petzl Universo. If you use a standard carabiner, check frequently that it is loaded correctly.

BELAY DEVICE USED INCORRECTLY

Examples of incorrect use of the device include not taking the rope in correctly on a standard belay plate and misusing an alternative device such as a Petzl Grigri by grabbing the release lever and pulling when the climber has fallen. This will result in him/her continuing to fall.

Solution Ensure you have read and understood the manufacturers' instructions and get some tuition if you don't understand them. Experienced climbers should guard against complacency.

USER ERROR – LETTING GO

Either through ignorance or complacency, people are frequently observed letting go of the braking part of the rope when belaying. You can't predict when a fall may occur and should be ready to hold a fall at any time. That means *never* letting go of the braking rope.

Solution Concentrate and don't *ever* let go. As a climber, if you ever look down and see your belayer not holding the rope, you know what to say!

LOWERING TOO FAST

Lowering too fast can result in losing control of the descent, the climber struggling to keep up with the speed of lower and potential rope damage due to the extra generation of heat through friction at the lowering point and at the belay plate.

Solution The belayer should retain control by lowering at an appropriate speed. Get training if

▲ Dangerous belaying – distraction can lead to the belayer letting go of the braking rope

▲ A light belayer may want to use a ground anchor

you are not sure how to do this. If you find it hard to lower someone in a controlled, make sure your belay plate is compatible with the thickness of rope you're using and ensure that the weight difference between the belayer and climber is not too great. Consider using a ground anchor if the belayer is lighter than the climber.

ROPE/BELAY PLATE INCOMPATIBLE

Ropes vary in thickness and belay plates vary in design and size. You must ensure that the two are compatible. A thick rope in a tight belay device could be very hard to take in and adjust, whereas a very thin rope in a slick belay plate could make holding a leader fall extremely difficult.

Solution Make sure that belay plate and rope are compatible. Take advice if required. It is a good idea to test new belay plate/rope combinations in a controlled situation before using them.

BELAYER STANDING AWAY FROM WALL

You often see belayers standing away from the wall, perhaps using the rope angle between them and the first bolt to reduce the force felt when lowering, or in the event of a leader fall. There have been a number of accidents in which the belayer has lost control as a result of standing too far away from the wall, particularly when there is also too much slack rope in the system and/or a lack of concentration. Standing away from the wall is acceptable for

experienced belayers in certain situations, but is best avoided by beginners.

Solution Until you have a lot of experience, adopt good practice and stand close to the wall and just to the side of the route.

TOO MUCH SLACK ROPE

A lack of knowledge or complacency can cause this. Too much slack rope means that the climber falls further than he/she needs to and the whole system – belayer included – is subjected to a much greater force than should be the case. When leading, too much slack can result in the leader falling further than intended which can potentially result in injury through hitting holds on the wall or from hitting the ground if the fall takes place low down.

Solution Make sure you understand the principles of belaying and keep the right amount of slack in the rope. Get trained to belay correctly, if you're not sure.

▲ This belayer is standing too far from the wall

▼ Correct belaying position

▼ This belayer has given a bit too much slack rope to the leader

⌃ Some walls, such as Kendal Wall, have landing zones marked to give you an idea of where lowering climbers will finish

LOWERING ONTO OTHER CLIMBERS

Sometimes people seem to be touching down all over the place, especially on the steeper sections of walls. As a belayer or spectator, you are in danger of having someone lowered on you.

Solution As the belayer, be aware of any other climbers standing beneath the lowering zone. As a climber being lowered always be on the lookout for people standing beneath you.

FAILURE OF EQUIPMENT

The failure of equipment in indoor climbing is a very rare occurrence and is normally linked with another problem. For example, the BMC Technical Committee reports an incidence of rope failure at an indoor climbing wall, which was caused by acid damage to the rope in question. If your equipment is up-to-date, within its serviceable life, looked after according to manufacturers' recommendations and used correctly, then the chances of failure are extremely low. Auto-belay devices have been known to fail in very rare instances. The climbing wall should also have an inspection regime.

FALLS

Leading

In addition to the general problems previously mentioned, the following apply specifically to lead climbing.

LEADER FALLS BACK INTO WALL

Many falls on indoor walls do not harm the falling climber, especially those that take place on overhanging sections. It is possible, however,

▲ A leader fall can result in swinging back hard into the wall

FALLS FURTHER THAN EXPECTED DUE TO SLACK ROPE

This is self-explanatory, but happens quite often in my experience. It can lead to problems for the belayer as the forces can be higher than they ought to be. Some climbers seem to see providing extra slack as a way of providing a dynamic belay and a gentler resulting fall, but dynamic belaying doesn't just provide more slack, it allows a controlled feed of extra rope in a progressive manner during the fall.

Solution Manage rope to avoid excessive slack and learn dynamic belaying.

FALLS WHILE REACHING TO CLIP LOW BOLT

On the first few bolts on a route, it is possible to have a ground fall if you are pulling rope up to reach the next clip and fall before it is clipped.

Solution Try to clip when you are passing or close to the bolt to avoid having to pull up a lot of slack rope. This applies particularly to the second and third bolts.

▼ Clipping the second or third bolt from a low position can result in a ground fall

to fall and swing back hard into the wall. There are several reasons for this. First of all, if the fall is short, especially when there is not much rope out to stretch and absorb the energy created in the fall, the climber can come to a halt fairly quickly and, in doing so, slam back into the wall with some force. Second, the climber may fall away from the wall due to the angle and position in which they fell. Finally, it is possible to fall back into the wall if the climber is ascending a feature such as a corner, and falls from one side of it back onto the other. Climber and bolt position will determine the likelihood of this happening.

Solution As the lead climber you should be aware of your position and the likely consequences of a fall taking place. As the belayer you should learn how to perform dynamic belaying and consider using that to cushion a fall in the right circumstances. You could also consider not falling off!

REPEATED FALLS ON SAME ROPE CAN LEAD TO HIGH-IMPACT FORCES

Something to be aware of is that each time a fall occurs, the rope stretches to absorb the shock. It takes time for it to contract again and regain its shock-absorbing properties. Repeated falls on the same piece of rope can progressively increase the shock-loading, as the rope can't absorb as much energy. This can lead to bigger forces being felt by the whole fall arrest system.

Solution After a significant fall, you should tie into the opposite end of the rope so that you are climbing on a fresh part of it. All rope manufacturers advise against repeated falls on the same part of the rope.

HITTING HOLDS WHILE FALLING

Some hand and footholds stick out more than others and you can hit them when falling. If hit with your feet, they can push your body into a different position and potentially turn you sideways or upside down.

Solution Be aware of the hold layout and try to avoid hitting larger holds if you know you are going to fall.

BOULDERING FALLS

As we all know, it's not the fall that hurts, it's the landing.

Bouldering areas are now almost universally well protected with bouldering mats, reducing the likelihood of injury. However, there have been many accidents in the past involving falls onto mats from bouldering walls, making this probably the most incident-prone aspect of indoor climbing, with ankles and wrists particularly susceptible to injury.

▲ Don't stand beneath other boulderers! Even if it is Dave Birkett!

▲ A well-designed bouldering mat with no joins and fitted flush to the contours of the wall

▲ Falling in an uncontrolled manner can result in injury

Solutions

Current safety standards should have eliminated issues involving mat design, but carry out your own checks to be certain. Down climb as far as possible, avoid jumping from the top of bouldering walls and learn how to land in a safe and stable position. Some boulderers still use the back up of a 'spotter' – someone standing behind the climber, ready to steady them if they slip. This can be useful in certain circumstances, especially with beginners, but you have to be very careful to avoid being landed on ... it hurts!

If you are predisposed to injury from potential falls or jumps onto matting – for example, due to a previous injury or due to age – you should avoid problems with high cruxes and difficult top-outs. Look out for problems with low cruxes and traverses. Some walls, such as Kendal, deliberately create problems on which falling off is less likely to result in injury, by laying out the problem and the crux moves at below wall-top level.

HOLDS SPINNING

Many years ago at the original Keswick Climbing wall, the smaller section of wall was frequently used for bouldering and soloing as well as for leading and top roping. At four panels high (approximately 4m), it was protected by a quite narrow section of dense black matting.

I was reaching for the top of the wall from an undercut and just before my top hand curled around the safety of the summit hold, the foothold I was on decided to spin. Due to the position I was in, I felt myself being hurled from the wall sideways and I landed on the matting as flat as I could get, belly down. I recall trying to stand up, but the wind had been well and truly knocked out of me. After a moment of panic I lost consciousness and the next thing I remember was waking in a lying position on the mat with my friend, Paul Cornforth, asking me if I was OK. I felt an absolutely unreal sense of calmness.

I tried to put a brave face on and continued climbing, but felt grim and soon had to stop. As is the case with climbers and accidents, we all made the best of it and managed to get a few jokes in, the favourite being that it had been a good job I landed on my belly or I could really have hurt myself! I felt dreadful for some time afterwards as well and was quite shaken.

Solution You can't check every hold you use, but sometimes you'll feel a hold move just a tiny bit under your hand or foot. If you do feel movement, stop climbing immediately and inform the wall staff, making sure no one else uses the hold until it is secured.

▾ Retightening a bolt following the discovery of a loose hold

Some pointers

Many climbing wall accidents could be avoided by adopting a few simple checks and principles:

- Use a buddy system to check harnesses are fastened correctly, knots are tied in the right way and belay plates are threaded and attached correctly before starting the climb.
- Get some training. If you're new to climbing or using equipment you're not familiar with you should always receive training in its use unless you are very experienced. This could be from other more experienced climbers or through an instructor.
- Pay attention. Make sure you concentrate on the climb and the climber – don't allow yourself to become distracted.
- Remember that the climbing wall is a high-risk environment, and be constantly vigilant to ensure that you and your climbing partner are safe.
- Anticipation and foresight are so important – as you become more experienced you'll be on the lookout for situations in which accidents can occur before they have a chance to develop.
- Keep up-to-date with accidents and accident prevention and learn from the experiences of others through the BMC website (www.thebmc. co.uk) and through other climbing related websites, such as ukclimbing.com.

10

INJURIES AND INJURY PREVENTION

with help from Aimee Roseborrough
and Maureen Flett

Injuries are common among indoor climbers and can be divided into two categories: those sustained while in the process of climbing, bouldering or training and those sustained as a result of a fall. However you acquire an injury, it's a definite pain in other places than the affected area! Injuries can keep you out of climbing for longer than you may think and can develop into long-term problems that will haunt you in later life.

Climbing injuries can be divided into 'chronic' or 'acute'. Chronic injuries such as tennis elbow result from overuse, while acute injuries occur as a result of a movement that overloads a body part, such as a muscle, ligament or tendon, and causes a tear or strain.

> ➤ Avoid dynamic moves until you have the strength to perform them

Injuries sustained in falls vary greatly. Leader falls can result in direct trauma from banging into holds or the wall or even from hitting the ground. Bouldering falls may lead to wrist and ankle injuries.

More than 80 per cent of climbing wall injuries fall into the overuse category and for most indoor climbers, overuse injuries to fingers, elbows, arms and shoulders pose the greatest threat.

➤ Competition in climbing is inevitable

WHY DO CLIMBERS GET INJURED?

There are many external factors in addition to the individual climbers' personal situation.

- Competition drives climbers to try harder routes on smaller holds and more dynamic problems with longer reaches, increasing the possibility of injury.
- Some climbers don't warm up enough.
- Many newcomers to climbing, with otherwise sedentary lifestyles, try dynamic and very athletic moves early on in their climbing career when muscles, tendons and ligaments have not developed sufficient strength.
- Some people are just more susceptible to injury than others.

THE MAIN TYPES OF INJURIES

The most common injuries are listed below along with information about causes and symptoms, recovery and prevention.

Elbow

TENNIS AND GOLFER'S ELBOW (LATERAL AND MEDIAL EPICONDYLITIS)

Cause and symptoms An overuse injury. The tendons of the hand and forearm all insert into points on the inside and outside of the elbow joint. Repeated use with insufficient rest results in degeneration of tendon tissues. Tennis elbow results in pain on the 'outside' of the elbow that often occurs while grasping objects and/or applying a turning force. Golfer's elbow results in a similar pain on the 'inside' of your elbow.

Recovery and treatment

- Ice 3–5 times a day for 10 minutes at a time.
- Treatment involves eccentric exercise, which is the opposite of the usual upward weight lifting motion. You use the non-exercising hand to help the exercising hand lift the weight and then slowly lower with only the exercising hand.
- For medial epicondylitis (golfer's elbow), use both hands to lift the weight (4–7kg) in a wrist curl and then slowly lower with only the injured hand. Do 10 repetitions, 3 sets, 2 times a day and take 2 days off a week.
- For *lateral* epicondylitis (tennis elbow), as above, but with the reverse wrist curl exercise.

⌄ Wrist curl: use both hands to lift, and lower with injured hand

▲ Wrist curl for lateral epicondylitis

ANTERIOR/DEEP ELBOW PAIN (BRACHIALIS TENDONITIS)

Cause and symptoms Deep pain in the front of the elbow.

Recovery and treatment For brachialis tendonitis, follow the above protocol as for tennis elbow, but with reverse bicep curls.

Avoidance As tennis/ golfer's elbow.

TRICEPS TENDONITIS

Cause and symptoms When the arms are repeatedly used to push the body higher such as in a mantleshelf movement, triceps tendonitis can become a problem. This occurs right above the bony part of your elbow.

Recovery and treatment

- Exercises for triceps tendonitis are: push-ups on your knees, then once you can do two sets of 15 without any pain, switch to normal push-ups.
- Dumbbell (triceps) kickbacks with a really light weight and do sets of 20.

Avoidance Warm up and warm down effectively, be alert for early signs of pain and act straight away. It's important to balance the strength between the wrist flexors and extensors. Climbing strengthens the flexors more than the extensors, so reverse wrist curls are a good exercise for injury prevention. It is also advised to stretch the forearms daily.

➤ Stretching the forearms

- French stretch. Stand with your fingers clasped together and your hands high above your head. Stretch by reaching down behind your head and trying to touch your upper back with one hand while pressing down on your elbow to increase the stretch. Keep your elbow pointing towards the ceiling. Hold this position for 20–30 seconds; repeat 5 times on each side.

Avoidance As tennis/ golfer's elbow.

Shoulder

For climbers, the most common shoulder injuries are rotator cuff strain and tendonitis.

ROTATOR CUFF STRAIN

Cause and symptoms Rotator cuff strain symptoms include pain while moving your arm above shoulder height in front and/or to the side of the body. Causes include long reaches and overhead Gaston moves.

Recovery and treatment

- Treatment begins with a minimum of three weeks rest for a mild strain and five to six weeks off for a severe strain.
- Ice 3 times a day for 10 minutes each time for 7–10 days.
- Consider taking some anti-inflammatories during the first 2–3 days. Once pain at rest has subsided, then start a lightweight-training programme to strengthen the rotator cuff muscles.
- These exercises include the full can, external rotation and rows and shoulder extension.
- If these exercises do not cause pain, then try climbing lightly. If pain occurs with climbing, ice and take anti-inflammatories afterwards. Take another week off and continue the exercises (without pain).
- Continuing to irritate a rotator cuff strain can cause the injury to turn into rotator cuff tendonitis.

▲ Full can

▲ External rotation   ▼ Rows and shoulder extension

Avoidance Ensure you are thoroughly warmed up and perhaps undertake lower level dynamic moves as part of your warm-up. Ensure your fitness and muscular development match the type of dynamic moves you are attempting.

A rotator cuff strengthening programme can help prevent shoulder injuries. Exercises include 'full can', internal and external rotation, shoulder extension, military press, lower trapezius strengthening and scapular retraction (rows). Shoulder injuries may benefit from elastic band or cable exercises.

▲ Internal rotation

▲ Lower trapezius strengthening

ROTATOR CUFF TENDONITIS

Cause and symptoms Symptoms include dull pain with activity that may get better as you climb, but comes back; stiffness in the morning, and worse pain in the evening after activity. Pain is usually located in the front of the shoulder and may travel down into the deltoid. Often caused by repeated use of the arm in an overhead position.

Recovery and treatment
- Exercises are the same as for rotator cuff strain, but add eccentric external rotation with cables.

▲ Adding external rotation with cables

- Again, ice and anti-inflammatories are good post-activity treatment to keep the inflammation under control. Tendonitis can be difficult to eliminate.
- If there is no improvement after resting and trying these exercises, then consider seeing a physiotherapist.

Avoidance If you have any shoulder pain as a result of a rotator cuff strain, make sure that you allow recovery to take place.

Fingers

Finger joints are not designed to take our bodyweight, and structures such as the cartilage, ligaments and tendons are particularly susceptible to damage in certain positions and with certain techniques – a one-finger pocket is an example of this.

ANNULAR LIGAMENT TEAR

Cause and symptoms Acute injuries often involve the annular ligaments (pulleys). The pulleys hold the finger flexor tendon against the bone and prevent 'bow stringing' of the tendon. The most commonly injured pulley in climbers is the one at the base of the finger (A2). Pulley injuries often occur, for example, when a foot slips while the hand is crimping. This results in localised pain where the finger meets the palm (if an A2 pulley is involved). Pulley injuries are often graded by severity from a Grade I (strain) to a Grade III (complete rupture).

Recovery and treatment
- If you have a Grade III injury you need to seek medical care. Generally surgery is not necessary unless multiple pulleys are ruptured.
- For Grade II and Grade I injuries, a rehabilitation programme, including climbing, can be started after 2–6 weeks depending on the severity of the injury.
- Taping the base of the finger is strongly recommended for anyone who has sustained an A2 pulley injury when resuming climbing.

Avoidance Ensure fingers are warmed up well and have been used on a range of low pull-level holds of various shapes and sizes. Consider taping fingers for sessions involving high levels of crimping on small holds. Finger tendonitis can be avoided by paying attention to finger pain and balancing training with rest. If fingers are stiff and painful in the morning, more rest is required to allow for healing. Many injuries can be prevented by increasing rest intervals when the pain or discomfort begins.

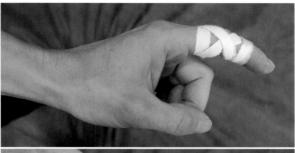

▲ Taping fingers for a return to climbing after injury

COLLATERAL LIGAMENT SPRAIN

Cause and symptoms Injury to the ligaments that run on either side of the finger joints often occurs when the foot slips and a climber's finger is in a pocket. This injury results in pain on the side of the finger joint and can be on one or both sides of the finger.

Recovery and treatment
- If there is instability at the joint, it should be splinted for 1–4 weeks. Then 1–4 weeks of rest should follow.
- Climbing can be resumed after 3–6 weeks on open-hand grips. Difficult lateral movement should be avoided. The joint should be taped prior to climbing.
- After a complete rupture of a collateral ligament, chronic joint instability may result and may require surgery.

Avoidance As annular ligament tear.

TENDONITIS

Cause and symptoms Chronic finger injuries include tendonitis of the tendon that flexes the fingers. This injury often occurs from climbing too much on small holds or climbing on an acute injury too early in the healing process. Pain is often felt at the base of the finger and may radiate into the palm or even forearm in severe cases. In the case of chronic injuries, the time frame for resting is dependent on how long the injury has been present. The longer the duration of the injury, the longer the rest interval will need to be for recovery.

Recovery and treatment

- Treatment for all finger injuries follows a similar protocol.
- Immediate treatment includes icing for 10 minutes, 3–5 times a day for at least the first 72 hours.
- Anti-inflammatory medications may be used during these first 3 days as well.
- Make a gentle fist with the fingers to increase blood flow to the fingers. Repeat this exercise 20 times, 5 times a day as long as it doesn't cause or increase pain. Gently stretch your forearms to help relieve some of the stress on the finger tendons.
- When you return to climbing, start on big holds well below your normal climbing level.
- If you have any pain, stop climbing, ice and rest for 5–7 more days before trying again.
- If you do not have pain, gradually increase the difficulty of what you are climbing but do not return to small holds for at least 6–8 weeks.

Avoidance An overuse injury – you'll need to try to identify it early and take appropriate rest. A varied climbing programme using a range of hold types, wall angles and range of difficulty will also help avoid tendonitis.

Neck

HYPEREXTENSION (ALSO KNOWN AS 'BELAYER'S NECK')

Cause and symptoms Hyperextension of the neck due to looking upwards can lead to muscle strain and tension. This is common in people who belay and is often referred to as 'belayer's neck'. It's really painful and can interfere with other aspects of your life.

Recovery and treatment

- Avoid belaying and other movements and activities that require looking upwards.
- Undertake gentle neck stretching exercises.

Avoidance Share out belaying duties and choose belaying positions that minimise neck pain. Consider using belaying glasses. Belaying glasses allow you to look straight forwards while still observing your climbing partner above you, by using a lens that bends the light through 90 degrees.

▾ Belaying glasses

Knee

The knee is a really complex joint, susceptible to a wide range of impact, twisting and exercise injuries. One injury is more specifically connected with climbing.

MENISCUS TEAR

Cause and symptoms Injury can result from moving up from the 'frog' position – where the knees are flexed and the leg is turned out – as well as very high-stepping moves. Excessive pressure through the knee joint when it is twisted at an angle in such moves can create a meniscus tear, which often requires arthroscopic surgery.

Recovery and treatment

* Recovering from a meniscus tear requires time and a gradual rehabilitation, although some recipients of arthroscopies report very quick recovery times. Much depends on the treatment required during the operation.
* Specialist advice should be sought following the operation.

Avoidance Thorough warm-ups always help, as will greater flexibility. Though it's not possible to avoid the types of movements that can cause knee injuries when climbing, performing them in a controlled manner and avoiding continuing through a move when pain is evident will help to avoid more serious injury.

PRINCIPLES FOR AVOIDING INJURY

Warm-up

An effective warm-up routine reduces the chance of both acute and chronic injury. Warming up ensures that joints have their full range of movement through the production of lubricating synovial fluid. It prepares the circulation by reducing the viscosity of the blood so that muscles have greater elasticity and increased contractile properties, and performs other important tasks, such as softening cartilage.

Take it easy and don't be afraid to rest

Don't push yourself to the limits every time you go climbing. If your muscles are tired, continuing to climb can cause injury by straining muscles and overusing tendons. Vary the intensity and type of your climbing, vary the duration and listen to your body – be prepared to rest and indeed build in rest days if you're training hard – you'll need them. Rest periods not only allow your body to recover, but are required to build better performance.

Anti-inflammatory drugs

The use of anti-inflammatory drugs such as Ibuprofen and Voltorol is very common to reduce joint pain and swelling. Their use may be an important part of your overall strategy for recovery from injury. However, you should take advice from a doctor or pharmacist before using them especially if you suffer from asthma.

Some anti-inflammatory drugs aggravate the stomach lining.

Some anti-inflammatories can cause mood swings and may have other side effects.

There is some evidence that anti-inflammatories actually hinder the healing process as their action stops the natural inflammation process that releases the necessary chemicals to start the proliferation and other stages of healing.

Variety is the spice of climbing

There's lots of variety to be had at most climbing walls – it's a great idea to use it. Climb lots of different types of route – slabs to get your legs working and flexible, technical vertical walls to develop stamina and skill, overhangs for power and technique, and so on. You'll probably find you favour certain styles of climbing and route types. If so, you should deliberately climb other types of route and problems, working on what you find hard. This is not only good for developing climbing skills. It will also help you to resist injury by providing you with better all-round strength and fitness.

Support your local tendons

Tendons – the connective tissue that attach muscles to bones – are particularly susceptible to injury by climbing. Use strips of tape to support your fingers (see finger injury section above) and avoid too many hard crimping moves.

Cross-training

Cross-train and do other sports. Cross-training will make you a more complete athlete and develop other muscles that help balance out your physical development, help you climb better, and equally importantly, avoid injury. Cycling, other mountain sports such as skiing and boarding, running, and so on, can all add to your overall fitness and ability to climb injury-free.

Avoid extreme climbing moves

Some types of climbing movements place much more stress on your body than others. Extreme moves that can cause problems include dynos.

Use big holds

Avoid routes with small finger holds and you will mostly avoid finger injuries. Clearly high-standard and competition climbers will have to use smaller holds, but even at that level, a considerable amount of training is performed on larger holds.

If it hurts – stop

If you feel pain in a finger, elbow or shoulder, for example, stop climbing immediately; if you're on a route, lower off. If you have any sign of injury, then immediately stop climbing. Don't continue by climbing easier routes; assess the injury and act accordingly.

Give it time

All injuries require time to heal – especially those to body parts with poor blood supply such as tendons. Recovery can take weeks or even months. If you're injured, take professional advice and don't rush things. It's a bit clichéd now, but do listen to your body – we all have different rates of healing depending on age, fitness, and so on, so get yourself a recovery programme and follow it, adapting as required along the way.

WARMING UP

Current research suggests that warming up ensures all joints such as the shoulders, hips and knees have their full range of movement by increasing the production of lubricating synovial fluid. Warm-up exercises prepare the circulation by reducing the viscosity of the blood so that muscles have greater elasticity and increased contractile capabilities.

Mild cardio-activity, such as running on the spot, needs to be done to raise body temperature and increase the heart rate.

Warm-up exercises should involve every part of the body, especially the hands and upper limbs, and should replicate the type of actions you will need to perform, but at a much-reduced intensity. An example of this would be climbing an easy route.

Avoid static stretches as a warm-up because these will have the effect of temporarily relaxing soft tissues.

The purpose of warming up is to help you climb better and reduce the likelihood of injury. Some readers may shudder at the thought of performing a full-blown warm-up routine in front of everyone at a busy climbing wall. Others may simply find it all too much effort and feel comfortable with a few waves of the arms, touching the toes a couple of times – or ankles if the toes are a bit far – followed by a quick rub of the hands with the dual benefit of warming them up and getting a bit of chalk to stick.

You have to put your prejudices about warming up to one side and adopt this routine, so you need to find a way that suits your own personality and situation. For example, to raise your heart rate at the start of a warm-up you could jog outside rather than run on the spot in front of everyone else at the wall; even your stretches could be done in a quiet place outside. Basically, you need to find a set of exercises that work as a warm-up, and you need to find a place to perform them in which you feel comfortable.

IDEAS FOR WARM-UPS

Raise your heart rate

Get your heart and lungs working by raising your pulse for approximately 5 minutes by jogging, cycling, short sprints interspersed with walking, skipping, chasing your dog – or whatever other pulse-raising activity you feel comfortable with. You'll increase blood flow, warm the muscles and soften joint cartilage in preparation for the impacts of strenuous exercise.

Prepare to stretch

Before you start to really stretch the individual components of your body, make sure you allow them to rotate and move in a full normal range of motion. At this point you're not stretching them, just making sure everything has been allowed to work through its full range. Hip circles, arm rotations, finger clenches, wrist rotation and gentle leg lifts to the front, back and sides are all examples of this part of the warm-up.

Stretch

By this point your heart and lungs are working harder and your joints have already exercised within their normal range of movement. Stretches should feel comfortable and should not be forced too much, as that could result in injury. Warm-up stretches should not be static, so introduce some dynamism into your stretching, while avoiding the violent bouncing movements you sometimes see. For example, in the exercises listed below, the 10-second holds should include some gentle movement at the tight point of each one.

Fingers Rub your hands together and wriggle your fingers. Gently rotate your wrists. Place your hands in the prayer position and lower them at the same time as you raise your elbows. Gently stretch each digit backwards and forwards. Grip some different shaped holds quite tightly to prepare your hands for using them.

⌄ Stretching in the prayer position

Arms and elbows Hold one arm out straight in front of you and hold the fingers with your spare hand. Bend your wrist and fingers back, hold for 10 seconds and repeat 3 times for each arm. Hold onto an undercut hold or underneath an object with your hand flat. Use your other arm to gently push upwards at just below elbow level and feel your lower forearm muscles stretch out. Hold and repeat as before.

Shoulder and upper arm Hold your elbow and bring your upper arm behind your head, applying gentle downward pressure. Hold your arm out straight in front of you and then move it sideways across your body until it starts to stretch out as if you're doing the breaststroke. Place your arm across your chest, then hold your elbow with your other hand and gently pull it across. Hold and repeat as for previous stretches.

Back Stand legs apart and slightly bent, then lean sideways stretching your arm over your head (left arm over head if you're bending to the right). You'll feel the tension in your sides. Place the other hand on your hip or thigh for support. Stand with your feet apart and gently reach down towards your toes, allowing the weight of your upper body and arms to perform the stretch. This will stretch your lower back and also your hamstrings. Stand feet apart, put your arms straight out in front of you and rotate both with and without rotating at the waist. As with prior exercises, hold for about 10 seconds and repeat 3 times.

Legs Lift your foot up behind you and hold it with the hand of the same side. Gently pull the foot upwards and you'll feel your thigh muscles stretching. Hold in a comfortable, but slightly stretched, position for 10 seconds; repeat as above. Stand with your legs apart and reach to the ground with your hands. Hold and repeat. Then, reach to the left toes and then the right toes, hold each and repeat.

Climb

Now you can invest some time in warming up by enjoying some climbing at last! The basis of this part of your warm-up is to copy the activity you're going to do, but at a lower level of difficulty and intensity.

Try to use as many types of handholds and get into as many body positions as possible during your warm-up climbing, all of which will ensure the most specific types of movement have been incorporated. Start with easier climbing of a style similar to that you're aiming for and build up, always stopping short of maximum effort.

At this stage, rest for a while – perhaps 10 minutes before commencing your main climbing session – and consider light stretching before you start again.

A successful warm-up will leave you feeling ready to climb, loose and strong. If you 'overcook' your warm-up, you can end up not being able to perform at as high a level as you did in your warm-up routine. If this happens, you'll need to reduce the level of difficulty, duration and intensity of your warm-up.

COOLING DOWN

During climbing, many of the body's muscles will have been in a contracted state for long periods of time, and cooling down is vital to help muscles and soft tissues return to their previous state, lubricate the joints and decompress the spine. There is evidence that stretching after sport reduces the effect of Delayed Onset Muscle Soreness (DOMS). Much different to the warm-up routine, the cool-down needs to include plenty of static stretches, especially of the fingers, hands and upper limbs. The spine can be decompressed by lying on the floor, hugging both knees toward your chest and gently rocking for a few minutes.

GENDER- AND AGE-SPECIFIC PROBLEMS

Youth

Climbing requires power and power requires muscles. A growing body is interested in skeleton first, muscle later. This is more evident in young men, when rapid and uneven growth spurts result in a lot of tension at the tendon attachments to bones. Young men often need to do much more post-training and specific stretching at this time.

Fingers do not stop growing until you are approximately 16 years of age. This means growth plates are still active and are 2–5 times weaker than the surrounding tissues. This puts young climbers at risk for finger injuries that could result in long-term deformities and/or decreased range of motion. For this reason, it is suggested that climbers younger than 16 do not participate in intensive finger, hangboard or campus training. Finger pain in young climbers should not be ignored and requires immediate medical consultation.

Growing does require a lot of energy and, more importantly, rest. Therefore, it is vital to maintain a balanced training programme, allowing adequate rest days, but also taking into account school and college sporting activity.

Older climbers

Older, experienced climbers perhaps have some advantages in the injury stakes in that their joints and muscles are prepared for the types of activity expected from them. However, injuries sustained by older climbers take longer to heal and will develop more easily into chronic conditions. It is therefore important to treat injuries immediately and to be very careful not to aggravate them by climbing again too soon.

Older climbers who are new to the sport should allow time for their bodies to adjust to the requirements of climbing and take on more difficult levels slowly. Once again, any slight injuries should be allowed to heal to avoid them developing into chronic conditions.

Note The information contained in this section is based on current best practice, but please remember that continuing research and development can lead to new approaches and ideas and what's best practice now could be obsolete in a few years' time. It's therefore recommended that you use this section in conjunction with expert, up-to-date advice from your doctor or physiotherapist. The author and the contributing authors have provided up-to-date information in good faith, but cannot be held responsible for any problems of any sort arising from following the advice contained in this book. You are advised to use the information provided in conjunction with appropriate expert medical advice.

For further information from Aimee Roseborrough see www.climbinginjuries.com and from Maureen Flett see www.sportsphysio.com

11

QUALIFICATIONS

As indoor climbing has developed as a sport in its own right, a range of training and award schemes have developed to provide appropriate qualifications.

These are administered by Mountain Training UK and by NICAS (National Indoor Climbing Awards Scheme), with workshops offered through the British Mountaineering Council.

The Mountain Training UK awards – Climbing Wall Award and Climbing Wall Leading Award are designed for those who want to take on the responsibility for teaching others. A newly developed Climbing Coach Award scheme offers an alternative route to helping develop others' climbing skills, while NICAS is aimed at personal development.

No one needs to take an official qualification to climb at an indoor climbing wall, or at an outdoor venue for that matter. However, if you want to supervise others at a wall you'll need to go down the route of gaining the appropriate qualifications. NICAS provides an excellent way for younger climbers to develop their skills and knowledge in an organised way and other newcomers to climbing walls might find it useful.

THE NICAS SCHEME

NICAS is a UK-wide scheme designed to promote climbing development and accredit individual achievement on artificial climbing structures. It can be used as a starting point for people wishing to take up climbing and mountaineering. It is open to all candidates aged 7 and older.

▲ National and local climbing wall award and training schemes are great for encouraging young climbers to learn properly

Aims of the scheme

- To develop climbing movement skills and improve levels of ability.
- To learn climbing rope-work and how to use equipment appropriately.
- To develop risk assessment and risk management skills in the sport.
- To work as a team, communicate with, and trust a climbing partner.
- To provide a structure for development, motivation and improved performance.
- To develop an understanding of the sport, its history and future challenges.
- To provide a record of personal achievement.
- To point the way to further disciplines and challenges in climbing beyond the scheme.

Structure of the scheme

The scheme comprises five levels of award aimed at complete novices up to expert climbers. The scheme is split into two parts and takes a minimum of 100 hours to complete in its entirety. The five levels are:

FOUNDATION CLIMBER

An entry level aimed at novices that recognises their ability to climb safely under supervision.

TOP ROPE CLIMBER

Aimed at promoting good practice in climbing and bouldering unsupervised on an artificial wall.

TECHNICAL CLIMBER

A more advanced top roping and bouldering level that focuses on developing technique and movement skills.

LEAD CLIMBER

Concentrates on the skills required to both lead climb and belay a lead climber.

ADVANCED CLIMBER

The top level focuses on improving performance, a deeper understanding of climbing systems and the wider world of climbing.

⌄ Coaching and training through the NICAS scheme progresses to tackle some tough climbing

MOUNTAIN TRAINING AWARDS

The number of individuals who are introduced to climbing on walls has expanded enormously in recent years. Mountain Training UK (MTUK) have devised the Climbing Wall Awards to ensure that high standards of supervision are maintained, safety techniques are up-to-date and practised and that participants may be coached in such a way that both enjoyment and safety are enhanced whilst personal abilities are developed.

CWA (CLIMBING WALL AWARD)

The Climbing Wall Award scheme is for climbers who are in a position of responsibility when supervising climbing activities on indoor or outdoor climbing walls, artificial boulders and towers. It is primarily concerned with ensuring good practice, leading to the safe enjoyment of climbing activities, and to an understanding of the sport. It covers the supervision and management of activities such as bouldering, the teaching of basic movement skills and roped climbing, excluding the teaching of leading.

An additional module is available for those candidates wishing to supervise abseiling and top-roping activities on those walls that have top access.

CWLA (CLIMBING WALL LEADER AWARD)

The CWLA was designed to train and assess those who want to teach lead climbing skills on indoor or outdoor artificial climbing walls and structures with fixed protection. This includes a wide range of structures (including, for example, towers and mobile climbing walls). The award is concerned with ensuring good practice when developing

▲ Coaching young climbers can allow them to operate increasingly independently

leading skills. It covers the introduction, coaching and on-going development of the technical and movement skills required to lead routes. It builds on the skills acquired in either the Climbing Wall Award or the Single Pitch Award, one of which candidates must hold to access the CWLA scheme.

FUNDAMENTALS

The British Mountaineering Council runs a series of workshops that aim to provide instructors with the skills and knowledge to deliver training in movement, coordination, balance, and so on, to children. The FUNdamentals programme is used in other sports as well and is aimed specifically at enhancing a range of generic skills such as those mentioned above, which will help a young person to become increasingly proficient physically in his/her chosen sport.

The scheme also looks at the way in which it is possible to take advantage of 'windows of opportunity' presented during a young person's development in order to maximise their potential.

The BMC workshops are split into three levels that increasingly introduce climbing technique alongside the basic movement skills and are especially useful for instructors and coaches offering their services to young people.

Climbing Coach Awards

Mountain Training UK are also developing and launching a new Coaching Awards Scheme for 2013. This will be at two levels – Level 1 (Assistant Coach) and Level 2 (Coach). Further details can be found from the sources listed below for this, as well as the CWA and CWLA.

Mountain Training
Siabod Cottage
Capel Curig
Conwy LL24 0ET
Tel: +44 (0)1690 720272
www.mountain-training.org

An overview of the climbing qualifications set up can also be found through Mountain Training UK and also through the British Mountaineering Council, who runs a range of additional workshops including the FUNdamentals programme. Its contact details are as follows:

BMC
The Old Church
177-179 Burton Road
West Didsbury
Manchester, M20 2BB
Tel: +44 (0)161 445 6111
Fax: +44 (0)161 445 450
www.thebmc.co.uk

Further details about NICAS are available at:

Anne Garnish
NICAS Finance and Administration
c/o Mile End Climbing Wall
Haverfield Road
London E3 5BE
Tel: +44 (0)7768 441435
www.nicas.co.uk

12

COMPETITION CLIMBING

No matter what any old-timer climbers may say to you, climbing has always been competitive.

In general adventuring terms, reaching the Poles was competitive. In mountaineering, climbing the Eiger Nordwand for the first time or making the first ascent of Everest was competitive. The only difference was that generally the competitors were competing at different times – in separate races if you like, rather than in the same race.

There was competition to make the first ascent of Mont Blanc and the Matterhorn, and you can't tell me that Victorian climbers weren't competing with each other – albeit in a most 'gentlemanly' way – to make first ascents of the classic British rock climbs.

I've heard stories of spontaneous bouldering competitions in the 1950s and there's plenty of evidence of climbers competing against each other to make the first ascents of particularly coveted rock climbs.

CLOSET COMPETITION

Most of this competition was hidden, although it lay just beneath the surface with only the main protagonists aware of the sport's true competitive fierceness.

˅ A modern IFSC competition taking place against the background of the Mont Blanc massif – itself the scene of intensive competition to make the first ascent of Mont Blanc

▲ St Peter's Square – most climbers in the 1960s and 1970s would have choked on their spam sandwiches had they seen this as a vision of climbing in the 2000s!

So climbing has always had this notion of 'closet competition' and many climbers in the 1960s, 1970s and into the 1980s were very much against the concept of making climbing an overtly competitive sport. I recall there being a very strong feeling among climbers against introducing competitive climbing for fear it would commercialise and regulate a sport noted for its anarchic roots and distinct lack of rules and regulations.

In fact, many climbers openly scoffed at the idea of climbing competitions, but this was, in most cases, simply a way of trying to protect their own coveted vision of the sport as something mysterious and different, secretive even, with its own closed society, its unwritten ethics and code of practice. I suspect many climbers simply did not want climbing to become a mass-participation sport and thus lose its romantic identity.

They thought climbing would never become a competitive sport. They were wrong.

THE BEGINNING OF ORGANISED COMPETITION

Organised competitions started in the late 1940s in the USSR as speed climbing events. These took place outside and were often run with a pulley at the top of the climb that wound in a cable or rope as the competitor climbed. The competitions stayed within national borders until 1985 when the first organised European speed climbing event was held at Bardonecchia in Italy. This, and the following year's event in Arco, attracted thousands of spectators and several TV stations. The final rankings placed French superstars Catherine Destiville and the late Patrick Edlinger in pole positions, providing an extra gloss to the events and cementing the place of competitions in the climbing world.

The events were not held without criticism though and there were concerns about damage to the natural environment, which led, in the following years, to events becoming established on artificial

▲ Competitors and spectators alike enjoy the climbers topping out

walls only. This was clearly an inspired move, not only eliminating fears of environmental damage on natural crags, but also allowing the creation of routes to set standards on walls which would be built in ever more complex and imaginative ways.

I recall this period of climbing development and very clearly remember watching my first competitive climbing competition at an outdoor show in London in the late 1980s. The final route had been set for the qualifying competitors and I watched several excellent climbers force their way to a high point about 3m below the top of the wall – but there was a real stopper move there and no one could get past it until there was one climber left – Jerry Moffatt. He climbed to the high point with a casual ease, and, pausing for dramatic effect, flashed the final couple of moves to leap for the final hold in a piece of dramatic showmanship that had everyone cheering and shouting. It made great viewing and for me, it showed very clearly that competitions were here to stay.

INTERNATIONAL COMPETITION

At an international level, here's how competition climbing has developed.

- In 1991, the first World Championships were in Frankfurt, Germany, an event that now takes place every two years.
- In 1992, the first World Youth Championship took place in Basel, Switzerland, immediately demonstrating the attraction sport climbing holds for young people, and becoming an annual event.
- In 1997, a new body, the ICCC (International Council for Competition Climbing) was created inside the UIAA, in order to guarantee autonomy to the sport and to provide it with the tools for its development, and in 1998 the new discipline of bouldering was officially introduced.
- In 2005, Competition Climbing was successfully introduced in the Duisburg World Games, as well as in the Asian Indoor Games.
- In 2006, the Union Internationale des Associations d'Alpinisme (UIAA, more commonly known as the International Mountaineering and Climbing Federation) decided to stop its involvement with competitive climbing, and a new organisation – the International Federation of Sport Climbing (IFSC) was founded in 2007.
- In 2007, the International World Games Association (IWGA) accepted the IFSC and confirmed that climbing would form part of the 2009 Kaohsiung World Games.
- On 10 December 2007, the International Olympic Committee (IOC) granted provisional recognition to the IFSC, welcoming sport climbing into the Olympic Movement and on 12 February 2010, the IOC granted definitive recognition to the IFSC, now part of the Olympic Family.
- On 4 July 2011, the IOC Executive Board decided to include sport climbing in the shortlist (together

with seven other sports) for a possible new sport to enter the 2020 Olympics. If climbing gains Olympic status it will herald some major changes in the way in which indoor climbing competitions are run and organised in Britain and it will have an equally major impact on the training and development of young climbers – and, almost inevitably, on participation levels.

The IFSC now has over 80 country members and says the sport has gained credibility, not only because of its spectacular competitions, but also for its social values, as seen by its introduction as a curriculum sport in many countries. The rapid development and growth recorded in many developing countries proves that climbing has a great future as an alternative, spectacular activity for people of all ages to enjoy.

It's also worth noting that there has been a huge increase in disabled athletes participating in competitive climbing. Paraclimbing is now well established with a high standard of competition.

THE MAIN DISCIPLINES
There are now three principal disciplines.

Lead climbing
Climbers have to lead routes of a certain standard to qualify and the finals involve tougher climbs, the winner being the one who gets to the top or reaches the highest point. At national and international level these routes are extremely difficult and competitors are subject to strict regulations.

Speed climbing
How fast can you get to the top? That's the only thing that really counts. The routes might be easier than for the lead climbing competitions, but they're still tough. The Russians were doing this on real crags in the 1940s!

◄ Russia's Dinara Fakhritdinova competing in the Indoor World Climbing Championships 2012 in Paris

➤ Jain Kim of South Korea, 2012 World Champion Overall

Bouldering

Competitive in an unorganised fashion for many years for outdoor boulderers, indoor bouldering is now immensely popular and the sheer number of new participants should ensure that standards are pushed yet further in years to come.

⌃ Katharina Saurwein of Austria at the 2012 Boulder Worldcup in Munich

⌄ Just about anything goes in modern bouldering!

In Britain, the early development and establishment of climbing walls led to local competitions ahead of their time in the overall development of competitive climbing. This was particularly well-illustrated by the proliferation of local bouldering competitions that not only continue today, but have grown massively in popularity.

Competitive climbing is now well-developed in Britain, with the British Mountaineering Council (BMC) taking on responsibility for developing competitions with financial support from Sport England.

THE ORGANISATION OF COMPETITIVE CLIMBING

Starting top-down, this is how the competitive side of climbing is now organised – though this could change if climbing is accepted as an Olympic sport.

The IFSC – the world governing body – is responsible for running the World Championship which takes place every two years, the World Youth Championship, the Paraclimbing Championships and climbing at the World Games. These are all major international events. The latest World Championship had over 500 athletes from 56 countries taking part,

16,000 spectators and almost 130,000 daily viewers for the whole event.

Below this are the Continental Councils, for example, the European Council of Sport Climbing, responsible for the European Lead, Speed and Bouldering Championships at both senior and youth level.

At national level, the BMC is the representative and governing body for climbing and mountaineering. Long-established, with a great reputation for looking after the interests of outdoor walkers, mountaineers and climbers, the BMC is now fully behind competition climbing, and for anyone interested in competitions, their website (www.thebmc.co.uk) is a great source of information.

In Britain, we have a similar spread of lead, speed and bouldering competitions at national level, and for different age groups such as Junior, Youth and Senior, with the difference that British teams are selected as a result of performances in the respective events.

The BMC also oversees the annual BMC Leading Ladder – a grass-roots event with categories for different grade climbers. Routes are set at 37 different climbing walls throughout the country during different periods and you can simply turn up and climb them, recording your results on a scorecard. This is a great way to enjoy the competitive aspect of climbing without too much of a song and dance and, with the lowest category open to climbers operating between 5a and 6b, many regular wall users will be able to have some no-pressure fun.

Most climbing walls also have their own bouldering competitions or ladders, with many problems of different grades to go at over a set period of time. There are also regional bouldering competitions – details of both of these should be available from your local climbing wall.

Finally, if you get into bouldering with a few

▲ Bouldering competitions are easy to compete in and great fun

mates, you'll soon find that you're competing with each other quite naturally, inventing problems, setting variations and so on, so you can enjoy competitive climbing outside the organised competitions at any time.

Competition climbing has developed from its roots in Soviet speed climbing, the controversial outdoor European Competitions of the mid-1980s and the naturally competitive rivalry between climbers generally, to a sport with a highly organised local, regional, national and international competitive framework. When, as it surely will, climbing is given full Olympic status, it will herald yet another major push in the development of the sport, an impact likely to be felt strongly in Britain, but even more so in many emerging countries that don't have the same historical connections with climbing as we do.

Anyone want to take a bet on the 2032 Olympic Climbing Gold Medal being won by a climber from a country that doesn't even have a climbing wall yet?

13

CLIMBING
OUTDOORS

I've mentioned elsewhere

in this book that there has been a terrific change in the nature of indoor climbing. Many of the climbers I spoke to when researching it had never climbed outdoors and some walls estimated that between 80 and 90 per cent of their customers were exclusively indoor climbers. More traditional climbers may well frown at this, but what I came across was a vibrant and friendly atmosphere at the walls, in which lots of people were enjoying climbing.

Many of these newcomers who now climb on indoor walls will never want to climb outside. Some will mix indoor and outdoor climbing, while others will use indoor climbing substantially as a means of getting into and then improving their outdoor climbing standard.

The differences between indoor and outdoor climbing are many. To go outdoor climbing you leave behind the consistency of indoor climbing along with the relatively safe environment it offers. You leave behind the controlled temperature and dry, windless conditions. You leave behind the regular fixed bolts, the colour-coded climbs and artificial holds, the padded floor and handy café!

In its place you'll find wind, sun, rain and sometimes snow, an inconsistent territory full of objective dangers, wildlife to share the location with, natural rock features with no bolt-on holds, lots of cracks and, unless you're at a sport climbing venue, you'll find a lack of fixed protection and belays. For those brought up climbing on indoor walls, the great outdoors provides a combination of inspiration and apprehension. Only once you've tried it will you know whether you want to embrace it or whether you prefer the predictability, convenience and reliability of climbing indoors.

▾ Checking out the routes at Sennen Cove. Indoor walls haven't quite replicated the sea-cliff atmosphere yet

If you're one of those climbers who likes the idea of giving it a go outdoors, this chapter contains a rundown of some of the key skills you need to get started along with some advice on where to go, equipment, training and skills development.

If you've never climbed outdoors I'd urge you very strongly to give it a try. Go to a popular venue with a mix of bouldering and routes and take a look at what's going on. I've a sneaking suspicion that many of the newcomers to indoor climbing would love climbing outdoors. There is also the possibility that the new wave of indoor climbers will provide a real boost to outdoor climbing.

One of our greatest outdoor climbers, Dave Birkett, who appears a lot in this book, shares with me a great love of the outdoors – the wildlife, the weather and the fantastic scenery for example. However, when I asked Dave what makes outdoor climbing so special, his answer didn't involve any of those points.

For me it's about going to new and different places and meeting people. It expands your horizons and has a great social side. There's a simple truth in climbing that holds true in everyday life.

I'd concur with that – the nature of outdoor climbing does bring people closer than an evening at the wall, as the stakes are almost invariably much higher –the 'brotherhood of the rope', as it's been called. Climbing outdoors almost always takes place in beautiful and interesting surroundings and once your outdoor experience takes you abroad and into different cultures, it provides a wonderful learning experience as well.

MAKING A START

Though it's perfectly possible to go and enjoy some bouldering out of doors with little further knowledge than that required to boulder on an indoor wall, it's not really an option to try real

▲ Pete Munford teaching a group how to belay

climbing outdoors without the guidance of more experienced friends or without undertaking a course to give you some of the basic skills and knowledge required. You could also look to join a club – you might find one through your local climbing wall, or if you're at a university there could be one there. The BMC website is another good point of reference, with a list of clubs plus contact details.

My personal opinion is that it's best to do a course to start with, even if you have access to more experienced friends or a club. A course with a reputable guiding/instruction company will equip you with the right skills and knowledge to start your outdoor climbing in a safe way.

ABOUT ROCK CLIMBING OUTDOORS

Before you make a start it's worth understanding the nature of climbing outdoors, what the norms are, what to avoid and what you need to know. Unlike many sports, rock climbing outdoors has no rules and regulations and there is a great emphasis on taking responsibility for your own actions and safety.

Outdoor climbing can take different guises. For example, there is bouldering, lead climbing (traditional and sport), top roping and solo climbing. There's also winter climbing, Alpine and Himalayan routes and newer branches, such as dry tooling.

One factor, pointed out to me many times, is that to go outdoor rock climbing requires a much higher investment in time and money. Travelling to climbing areas can take many hours if you live in the south of England and the cost of fuel or public transport is high. You've also got to buy more equipment and learn how to use it. This combination of factors provides one of the most compelling reasons why so many indoor climbers don't make it to the great outdoors. I've added a note at the end of each section below to give some idea of the relative demands each form of climbing makes on your time and money.

BOULDERING

Bouldering is great fun and an ideal way of increasing climbing fitness and technical ability as well as being a fantastic branch of climbing in its own right – this is probably where many indoor climbers will start.

Many regular outdoor climbers have a bouldering session before or after going climbing, and many others go to outdoor climbing locations just to boulder. You don't need much gear and there are lots of places to go.

You'll find the most popular bouldering areas have their own guidebooks (or 'topos'), and the problems are well-documented in addition to being well chalked-up following any spell of dry weather. However you don't have to stick to what the guidebooks say. There are bouldering possibilities at the foot of and around most popular climbing crags – you just need a little imagination. Lots

▲ Bouldering at The Roaches in Staffordshire

of information is available through the internet and websites such as ukclimbing.com. Climbing guidebooks also usually mention key bouldering locations within the areas they cover. Bouldering is also very popular abroad, the best example being the remarkable and extensive boulder fields among the forests of Fontainebleau – or 'Font', as it is popularly known.

In terms of equipment, you'll need rock shoes and a chalk bag, a piece of towelling to keep your feet dry and clean, and a bouldering mat is recommended to help minimise the possibility of injury in the event of a fall. A toothbrush is useful to clean smaller holds, where excess chalk can build up and decrease the available grip, or to clean smaller and sloping footholds, where dirt can cause the same problem.

Bouldering is inherently dangerous. In the event of a fall there's no rope to hold you. The landings are not always flat – and vary between soft and sandy earth through to jagged and potentially limb-breaking rocks. The development of bouldering mats has helped to reduce injuries resulting from bouldering, but you should be aware that even using them, you still need to take more care than you would in most indoor situations. Check out the landing zone carefully and try to predict where you might land if you fall. Place your bouldering mat carefully to reflect this. Bouldering with friends and using more than one mat to protect a problem is commonplace.

Bouldering is the cheapest and easiest form of climbing to participate in.

TOP ROPING

Top roping outdoors is effectively the same as that on an indoor wall, except that there are no fixed ropes and no pre-fixed anchors to clip into. You've got to place the anchor points yourself, and depending on where they are in relation to the climb, you may top rope with the belayer on top of the crag or you may belay from the bottom as on the indoor wall. To top rope climb, you need a climbing rope, harnesses and belay plate as you would on an indoor wall, but you also need some equipment with which to set up anchors and possibly a short length (perhaps 10m) of static rigging rope to enable you to link anchors effectively and to position your rope correctly. Some formal instruction or help from experienced climbers is required to enable you to set up top ropes – you should not attempt to do this otherwise. Top roping is considered a secondary method of climbing to leading and you should be aware that the general etiquette is for top rope climbers to give way to those wanting to lead climb the same route. Some climbers look down on top roping as inferior, but the truth is that it's a great way of having a go at climbing outdoors on natural rock, so don't be afraid to do it – just don't monopolise the most popular climbs for hours on end!

To top rope outdoors you'll also need to have a guidebook for the area you're intending to climb in

and you'll need to stick with single pitch climbs – ideally starting off with shorter ones which follow a clean, straight line to the top of the crag.

Top roping requires some investment in equipment, training, guidebooks and in travelling to appropriate crags, so it starts to get quite a bit more costly than bouldering.

LEAD CLIMBING/FREE CLIMBING

Lead climbing is still reckoned by many to be the style of climbing to aspire to. As there are no bolts to clip on trad climbing areas, you have to learn how to use a variety of equipment to enable you to protect the climb – nuts, cams and slings, for example. Placing good protection and managing the run of the rope(s) while lead climbing is an art form and takes a long time to master.

▼ A lead climber on a classic V Diff, Tystie Slab at Reiff. You can probably see that there is little comparison between leading this and a similarly graded climb indoors.

In addition to climbing the route, you have to develop the skills and strength to find the best locations to place protection and then place it correctly so it will stop you if you fall. It's more tiring than top roping and there is the additional psychological pressure of having to climb not knowing the location of the next protection above you. The real-time danger levels are higher.

You need to invest a lot more physical and mental energy in leading a climb than top roping, but most climbers would say that the reward makes it well worthwhile.

A bigger financial investment is required for lead climbing. There's a more extensive range of equipment to be purchased along with a more significant training input, together with guidebooks and transport to crags.

SPORT CLIMBING

Sport climbing venues in Britain are nowhere near as commonplace as on the continent, but they do exist and are growing in number. Bolts are placed in situ as on indoor walls, though they may not be as close together, and lower-off points are generally provided. It's quite possible to move speedily from indoor climbing to outdoor sport climbing if your climbing grade is high enough – most sport routes in Britain tend to be in the higher grades.

Sport climbing is much more commonplace in other European countries, with southern Spain, Sardinia, Greece and France being particularly popular for British climbers, especially during the winter months. Low-cost flights coupled with cheap accommodation make a sport climbing holiday in many of these places seem very reasonable by comparison with a climbing holiday in Britain – and winter sunshine does you a power of good!

In theory, you can enjoy sport climbing with less financial commitment than traditional lead climbing as less equipment is required. You still need all the basics, plus rope and quickdraws, guidebooks and transport, so it lies somewhere between bouldering and traditional lead climbing in terms of time, transport and equipment costs.

▼ Sport climbing in Italy – great rock, bolts and blue sky!

▲ A typical modern, well-equipped via ferrata

▲ John White solo climbing Crimptyphon, E2 5c Compass Point

VIA FERRATA

A via ferrata ('iron way' in Italian) is a fixed path up a slope, generally provided by one or more steel cables attached to the rock face at intervals. Climbers scramble up using the cables for protection and a varying amount of fixed equipment such as rungs and bars. Started in the Dolomites following routes set up during the First World War and now very popular throughout the Alps, they are a great way for scramblers to experience big mountain crags, and a lot of fun for climbers as well.

SOLO CLIMBING/ FREE SOLO CLIMBING

Solo climbing is in many ways the purest way to climb, but the stakes are high – if you fall you're in trouble. Some climbers love soloing, but most don't

want to know. You need to be supremely confident and have enough experience to both judge the route against your ability and physical/psychological condition on the day, and to really understand the level of risk involved. This is only recommended to climbers with enough experience to make the crucial decisions required. Deep water soloing has become popular in recent years, though if you fall, the water isn't always soft or safe, and you need to know what you're doing.

This is low on cost, but high on risk.

WINTER CLIMBING

Some climbers progress to winter climbing, using ice axes, crampons, ice screws and a variety of other snow- and ice-related equipment in addition to some of the key climbing gear you'd use for rock routes. The levels of seriousness are notched up when you climb in winter. The weather is often poor, the nature of the climbing unpredictable and the environment harsh and often remote. The walk-ins can be long and arduous, protection on the routes less reliable ... and it's cold! You could be forgiven for thinking that it hasn't got much going for it – but the thrill of winter climbing, the often stunning nature of the scenery and the level of challenge you have to aspire to attract a lot of devotees.

You need to invest in more equipment and training than for other forms of climbing in Britain and, unless you live in the Scottish Highlands, you're likely to have to invest a lot more in transport costs and time too.

ALPINE CLIMBING

Climbing in the Alps can mean many different things – from easy snow plods to massive snow couloirs and icy north faces. You can climb purely on rock or enjoy the fantastic situations offered by a via ferrata. Most Alpine areas also offer great sport climbing and excellent bouldering alongside what's

⌃ Paddy Cave climbing on good ice in the Lakes

❯ Climbers on the Cosmiques Arête with Mont Blanc in the background

⌃ Mixed climbing involves a combination of dry tooling techniques, ice climbing and rock climbing

on offer on the bigger peaks.

Traditionally, climbers would learn their skills on the summer and winter crags of Britain, before transferring them to the bigger, mixed climbs of the Alps. In many ways the same holds true now – you need to acquire a broad range of skills on snow, ice and rock and learn how to cope with glaciated terrain and a more demanding overall environment.

Alpine climbing perhaps provides a classic example of how the greater investment in time, equipment, training and travel can be justified by the intensity and quality of the experience. You could easily forget a hundred single pitch climbs, but you'll always remember your Alpine routes.

The cost of Alpine climbing is high. A mix of winter and summer equipment is required, there are more training requirements, such as glacier travel and crevasse rescue. The transport and accommodation costs can also be high.

THE HIMALAYAS AND GREATER RANGES

Just as climbing in summer and winter in Britain provides a combination of skills useful for Alpine climbing, what you learn in the Alps helps to prepare you for climbing bigger mountains in the world's great ranges such as the Himalayas, the Andes or the Caucasus, for example. Only a small number of climbers will aspire to follow in the footsteps of Bonington and Scott, Messner, Diemberger and more recent luminaries such as Alan Hinkes and Kenton Cool, but those who do will be rewarded by a high-level quality of experience that justifies the levels of experience, training, commitment and cost involved.

AID CLIMBING

Aid climbing was popular – especially in America at one point. Bolts, pitons (pegs), slings and other assorted ironmongery were used for directly aided climbing. Some routes, on limestone crags such as Malham, were once predominantly aid climbs and at some other locations such as Millstone Crag in the Peak District, the superb finger cracks we climb free today only exist in that form due to early aid climbing with pegs. Times change, and many old aid climbs have been free climbed. The current emphasis is very much on free

climbing, and the use of pegs and bolts is mostly limited to very occasional protection, or to finding a way past an occasional blank piece of rock on an otherwise climbable route.

DRY TOOLING

Most things in climbing I get, but I'm not sure I really get the 'dry tooling' concept! Using axes and crampons to climb rock that doesn't have any snow or ice just seems a bit odd to me, but it does have plenty of devotees. It started on winter routes, where sections of rock had to be climbed in order to link together sections of ice, but has developed into a branch of climbing I'd describe as 'esoteric'. Then again, there's nothing wrong with that!

Dry tooling is quite common indoors now and is gaining popularity outside as small numbers of specific venues are developed. If you want to give it a try get down to your local wall and find out if they are offering sessions. It takes all sorts.

➤ Dry tooling in a Lake District quarry

Appendix

Rock climbing grading systems may well seem complex to start with. You'll probably find them a little confusing and hard to understand – join the club!

There are many different grading systems in use, relevant to the type of climbing you're doing.

The most important ones for indoor climbers are probably the French Sport Climbing system and bouldering grades, though it helps if you have an understanding of the grading system for British outdoor climbing.

OUTDOOR GRADING

Grading systems in the UK started in Victorian times, when climbs were given overall grades, such as Easy, Moderately Difficult, Difficult and Very Difficult. Though these are very easy grades by modern standards, at the time the early pioneers of rock climbing really meant what they described, and a Very Difficult route (V Diff in modern parlance) really was a climb of great difficulty for them.

As climbs became harder, the Severe grade and the Very Severe grades were introduced (it's not so long ago that the Very Severe (VS) grade in Scotland was as high as it went – though some of the routes graded at this level were in fact much harder). Beyond VS came the Hard Very Severe grade, and eventually Extremely Severe. This was later subdivided into E grades – E1 upwards in an open-ended system.

If we used this system (adjectival as it's called) exclusively it would only tell us part of the story about a climb's grade. How would we know for example if a route was not too difficult technically, but very dangerous and scary – or very tough for a couple of moves, but safe?

To provide more information on the nature of the difficulties on a route, a technical grade was introduced to sit alongside the adjectival grade. This technical grade went 3a, 3b, 3c, 4a, 4b, 4c, 5a, 5b, 5c etc., and it described how hard the toughest move on a climb was.

Take the VS grade for example. An average VS graded climb would have a technical grade of 4c. If it had an easier technical grade such as 4b, you would expect the route either to be very sustained, or lacking protection – making it more serious. If it had a harder technical grade such as 5a, you would expect the route to have a tougher than average move, but in a safe place – perhaps getting off the ground, or next to good protection. Therefore the British grading system for outdoor climbing, together with the guidebook description, tells you a lot about the nature of the difficulties you'll be faced with on the climb.

INDOOR GRADING

Outdoor and indoor sport climbing differs massively from the point of view that the climbs are bolt protected and therefore you don't have to worry as much about the level of seriousness of the climb. They can therefore be given a simpler grading system that only takes into account their physical difficulty, and walls generally use the French sport climbing system. Though this starts at 1, wall routes effectively start at 3, and work upwards with plus and minus adjustments to 5+, after which the grades are subdivided into a, b and c (for example 6a, 6b and 6c). After 6a, only plus symbols are used, e.g. 6b+. The current highest level of difficulty is about 9a.

Take a look at the comparison tables opposite to get an idea of how these grades relate to each other.

The reality is that it's almost impossible to compare the grade of an indoor sport route with a long, multi-pitch mountain climb, so it's perhaps best not to try!

For indoor routes, try different grades on different walls, and build up your experience of assessing grades – if nothing else it provides a lively topic for discussion in the pub afterwards!

Bouldering grades

To complicate things further, bouldering grades are also used, and these may differ from place to place. Some indoor walls use the British technical system, some the V Grade system and you'll even see Peak or Font systems being used.

Take a look at the grading tables to get some idea of how these grades compare, and when you're bouldering at the wall, you'll soon find out what grades you can climb at and from that point, the grades are just an indication of the relative difficulty of one climb compared to another.

LIMITATIONS

All grading systems have limitations, and perhaps the biggest one is how they relate to an individual's physical makeup and preferred style of climbing.

Some routes and boulder problems will appear significantly easier, or harder, simply due to the fact that your physique makes it so. There might be a very long reach for example, suited to tall climbers. There could be a move in which the crux hand and footholds are very close together and tall climbers find the move harder than shorter ones.

You might also find that your preferred style of climbing impacts on your ability to crack certain grades. You might be able to outperform your mate on slabs with small holds, but they might make you look like an eight stone weakling on those dynamic overhanging problems!

Like someone said to me at the wall recently: 'there's only two grades – those you can do and those you can't!'

My advice is not to get too hung up on grades to start with – just enjoy your climbing and find routes you can enjoy regardless of their grade.

COMPARISON OF CLIMBING GRADES

UK OVERALL	UK TECHNICAL	UIAA	FRENCH SPORT	AMERICAN
M	N/A	I TO II	1	5.1 - 5.2
D	N/A	II TO III+	1 TO 2+	5.2 - 5.3
VD	N/A	III TO III+	2 TO 3-	5.2 - 5.4
HVD	N/A	III+ TO IV+	2+ TO 3-	5.4 - 5.6
MS	N/A	IV TO IV+	3- TO 3+	5.5 - 5.6
S	4A - 4B	IV TO V-	3 TO 4	5.5 - 5.7
HS	4A - 4C	IV+ TO V	3 TO 4+	5.6 - 5.7
MVS	4A -4C	IV+ TO V	3+ TO 4+	5.6 - 5.7
VS	4A - 4C	V- TO V+	4 TO 5	5.7 - 5.8
HVS	4C - 5B	V+ TO VI	4+ TO 6A	5.8 - 5.9
E1	5A - 5C	VI TO VI+	5+ TO 6A+	5.9 - 5.10A
E2	5B - 6A	VI+ TO VII	6A+ TO 6B+	5.10B - 5.10C
E3	5C - 6A	VII TO VII+	6B TO 6C	5.10D - 5.11B
E4	6A - 6B	VII+ TO VIII	6C TO 7A	5.11B - 5.11D
E5	6A - 6C	VIII TO IX-	7A TO 7B	5.11D - 5.12B
E6	6B - 6C	IX- TO IX+	7B TO 7C+	5.12B - 5.13A
E7	6C - 7A	IX+ TO X	7C+ TO 8A+	5.13A - 5.13C
E8	6C - 7A	X TO X+	8A+ TO 8B+	5.13C - 5.14A
E9	7A - 7B	X+ TO XI	8B+ TO 8C+	5.14A - 5.14C
E10	7A - 7B	XI TO XI+	8C+ TO 9A+	5.14C - 5.15A

BOULDERING GRADES

V GRADE	PEAK GRADE	FONT	FONT TRAVERSING	BRITISH TECHNICAL
V0-	B0	3		5A
V0	B1	4		5A/5B
V0+	B1/B2	4+		5A/5B
V1	B2	5		5B/5C
V2	B3	5+		5C/6A
V3	B4	6A/6A+	7A	6A/6B
V4	B5	6B/6B+	7A+	6A/6B
V5	B5/B6	6C/6C+	7B	6B
V6	B6/B7	7A	7B+	6B/6C
V7	B7/B8	7A+	7C	6B/6C
V8	B8	7B	7C+	6C
V8+	B9	7B+	8A	6C/7A
V9	B10	7C	8A+	6C/7A
V10	B11	7C+	8B	7A
V11	B11/B12	8A	8B+	7A/7B
V12	B12	8A+	8C	7A/7B
V13	B13	8B	8C+	7B
V14	B14	8B+	9A	7B

Appendix CLIMBING COURSES

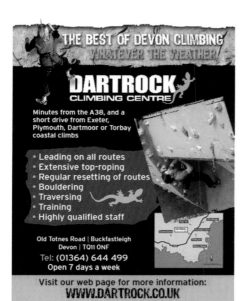

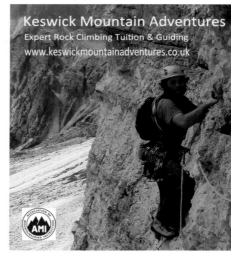
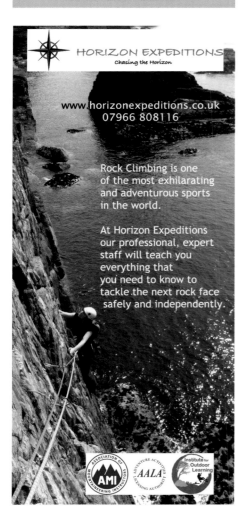

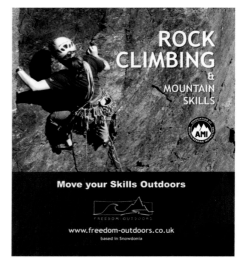

Glossary OF INDOOR CLIMBING TERMS

abseil The controlled descent on a rope, normally using a belay plate or specific abseil device.

arête A feature on a wall which pushes outwards like the spine of a book when it's held open at an angle of about 90 degrees, give or take a bit either way.

back and foot Technique for climbing chimneys in which your back is on one side of the chimney and you push your feet against the opposite wall.

bar As well as being the place most people head to after climbing, a bar refers to a specific technique. An arm bar, for example, involves spanning across a crack between palm and elbow, then using arm strength to create a twisting effect, which locks the arm across the crack.

barn door To swing round like a door opening – usually when you're in a layback position.

belay device A piece of equipment used to control the rope when belaying.

belaying The technique of operating a safety device to protect another climber.

beta Knowledge of a route that helps you to make the ascent.

bolt The term used to describe the fixed protection points in sport climbing. Bolts in real rock are basically big expansion bolts, securely fastened (though not universally so!). The bolt secures a hanger to the rock/wall that is then used to clip a quickdraw.

bouldering Climbing on boulders of real rock, on artificial outdoor boulders or purpose – built indoor walls. The climbs are relatively short and usually (but not always) low enough to jump back to the ground safely. See *bouldering mat*.

bouldering mat A portable shock-absorbing mat used to place beneath outdoor boulder problems to protect the climber in the event of a fall. See *bouldering*.

break A horizontal crack feature – literally a break in the rock face.

bridge To climb using hand and footholds on either side of a feature such as a corner or chimney. The holds on either side are used to push in opposition to each other.

bucket A huge handhold also known as a 'massive jug'.

bulge A rounded overhang.

campus board Overhanging board with wooden boards of different sizes attached horizontally. Used for pulling up from one to the next (or further) without using the feet, though some campus boards have footholds to help the weak. Some climbers swear by them for improving strength, others swear at them for ripping tendons! Not recommended for young, growing climbers.

campusing Climbing a route using only the hands in the style of using a campus board.

carabiner A metal clip with a sprung gate used to connect climbing equipment, ropes, etc., Also known as a 'crabs' or 'biners'. Sometimes spelt karabiner.

chalk Light magnesium carbonate – vital for improving grip, especially on sweaty climbing wall holds. Too much chalk on holds can have the reverse effect, which is why you'll see some climbers brushing the holds off.

chimney A fissure wide enough to fit your whole body into. See *bridge*.

clipping The act of clipping your rope into a quickdraw or your quickdraw to a bolt. See *extender*; *bolt*.

corner The opposite to an arête – like the inside of a book held open at 90 degrees.

crack A split in the rock face that could be at any angle to the rock or wall – diagonal, horizontal or vertical, for example. Very wide cracks form chimneys and as they get narrower form off widths, fist cracks, hand cracks and finger cracks. See *chimney*.

crater To fall and hit the ground, also known by other names according to region such as 'deck out', 'muckle gert thump'.

crimp A small hold onto which you can just get the ends of your fingers. To crimp is the action of locking your fingers off on a small hold.

crux The hardest move on a climb.

dead hang Also known as a 'straight arm hang', this refers to a relaxed position adopted when resting or clipping, with the arms straight and with the minimum required force used to hold the position.

dead rope The rope exiting the belay plate to the belayer's braking hand, then the ground. The live rope is the end of rope going from the belay plate to the climber.

disco leg Involuntary leg shake on a climb, that can be usually stopped by lowering the affected heel. Also known as 'Elvis leg'.

dogging Trying and failing to climb a route without falling or resting on the rope. Normally, the climber does not return to the ground, but simply rests and carries on. If the climber returns to the ground each time after falling it's called 'yo-yoing'.

dyno A dynamic leap or jump to reach a handhold, usually involving pulling with the arms and pushing with the feet in unison to jump high.

Egyptian A climbing move, where the hips are puller into the rock through a sideways twist and lock.

exposure The feeling of being at height, often associated with fear. Normally used as an outside rock climbing term, but can apply to big indoor walls as well.

extender A sling to which two carabiners are linked to extend a bolt or other protection and into which the rope is clipped when lead climbing. Also known as a 'quickdraw'. See *carabiner*.

figure-of-four An unusual climbing move increasingly used by competition ice climbers and dry toolers. A bit of a party trick and not used very much in reality.

figure-of-eight An 8-shaped metal device used for abseiling and belaying – popular on the continent, but not in Britain.

figure-of-eight knot The most common knot used to attach a rope to the climber's harness. Reliable, easy to learn and easy to check that it's tied correctly – recommended.

fingerboard A home-made or specially designed section of board, typically with holds of

▲ Quickdraws on a wall

different shapes and sizes and used to perform pull-ups and hangs.

flag To place a leg out sideways for balance.

flash To climb a route first time without falling, though you might have some prior knowledge and information (beta).

Gaston Named after legendary french climber Gaston Rébuffat, it involves pulling sideways on holds as if you were trying to open the doors of a lift.

grade A measure of how difficult a climb is. There are many different grading systems in use, and a degree course in understanding them can't be far away!

Grigri A belay device that locks when it is subjected to a sudden loading like a leader

fall. Very popular with sport climbers.

gripped Properly scared – often unable to move until the inevitable happens!

groove A feature in the wall or rock, shallower than a corner but well-defined.

headpoint The ascent of an outdoor rock climb following practice and possibly involving preplaced protection.

heel hook The use of your heel to pull down on a hold at a higher level – often head height.

jamming Climbing techniques involving placing body parts (usually hands, fingers, feet) into a crack to secure a hold.

jug A really big handhold.

layaway A handhold used by leaning sideways from it.

layback A technique for climbing using layaway holds, also known as 'sidepulls'. Laybacking technique is often used for ascending cracks or sharp arête features when both hands pull in opposition to the feet.

leader A term used to describe person climbing first, or 'leading' the route. In indoor climbing the leader lowers back to the ground after finishing the climb.

live rope The rope leading to the climber from the belay device.

lower off The fixed anchor at the top of the climb through which the leader clips their rope before being lowered down.

mantleshelf or mantle A

climbing technique used to establish yourself on a ledge – a good analogy is getting out of a swimming pool, when you straighten your arms in a downward push, lock them off and lift one leg out to stand up on. There is usually less water and a smaller hand ledge in real climbing!

match Also known as a 'share', you use both hands or a hand and a foot on the same hold.

monodoigt or mono A small hole or pocket in the rock or wall into which you can just insert (and if you're strong, pull on) one finger.

off-width The most difficult width of crack to climb – too wide to jam feet or hands and too narrow to get into. Not found much on indoor walls, if you struggle on off-widths take comfort from the fact that you're not alone!

onsight An onsight ascent is to climb a route bottom to top with no rests or other trickery, and without any prior knowledge – you just rack up and climb the route.

pinch A hold which can be pinched between thumb and fingers to get a grip.

pitch Single pitch climbs are done in one section. Multi pitch climbs are generally longer and done in two or more sections called pitches.

pocket A hole in the wall

▲ Adam Lincoln performing a 'Gaston' move with his right arm

or rock which can be used as a hold.

protection The in-situ protection clipped by leaders on walls and sport routes such as bolts, and climber-placed protection devices that climbers place and clip into on outdoor routes to minimise the consequences of falling.

pump Extreme forearm tiredness. Your forearm will feel tight and the strength in your hands will have all but disappeared due to the build up of lactic acid in the muscles.

quickdraw See *extender*.

red point Leading a sport route after prior inspection and even practising moves. It comes from the German word *rotpunkt*, which signifies a small red circle painted at the base of previously aided climbs when they have been free climbed.

roof Big overhangs – might be more appropriately called ceilings, but aren't!

runner A point of protection that allows the free movement of the rope through it. Each time you clip a bolt or a piece of natural protection on an outdoor climb, you're clipping a 'runner', short for running belay.

screamer A fall, often sudden and dramatic. Could be called a 'wazzer', a 'whipper' or a 'flyer'.

seam A vague and unpronounced feature on the wall or rock, like a crack that hasn't been finished.

sequence A specific series of moves required to overcome a section of climbing.

sharp end If you're on the sharp end of the rope you're leading.

slab A section of wall less than vertical, often sub-defined into eg steep slab, gentle slab. When slab angle reaches more than 70 degrees it is usually referred to as a 'wall'.

sloper A sloping hold that is often hard to hang onto.

smearing Flat-footing the sole of the rock shoe onto a sloping area of wall or rock, and gripping through friction.

solo Climbing without ropes. Very high risk but extremely satisfying and some would say the purest form of climbing. Many climbers disapprove. Solo climbing is not allowed on indoor walls.

sport climbing Climbing on bolt-protected routes.

static rope Low stretch rope not suitable for lead climbing on, but often used for abseiling.

taping up The use of tape, such as zinc oxide tape, around the fingers to protect tendons.

thank god hold A big hold that provides a rest following a series of sustained climbing.

top rope To climb with a rope above you.

▼ Nick Moulden holding a sloper

topping out Reaching the top of the climb.

traditional or 'trad' Normal climbing to most outdoor climbers, in which the lead climber places natural protection as they climb.

traverse To move across the rock horizontally or diagonally in either direction, rather than directly upwards.

undercut/undercling A hold that can be pulled from beneath to be used to best effect.

wired To have a route 'wired' means to have its moves completely worked out, usually by having done it a few times.

Index